MAKING **MONEY** MAKING **FURNITURE**

MAKING **MONEY** MAKING **FURNITURE**

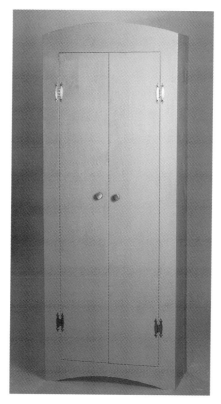

BLAIR HOWARD

POPULAR WOODWORKING BOOKS
CINCINNATI, OHIO
www.popularwoodworking.com

READ THIS IMPORTANT SAFETY NOTICE

To prevent accidents, keep safety in mind while you work. Use the safety guards installed on power equipment; they are for your protection. When working on power equipment, keep fingers away from saw tables, wear safety goggles to prevent injuries from flying wood chips and sawdust, wear headphones to protect your hearing, and consider installing a dust vacuum to reduce the amount of airborne sawdust in your woodshop. Don't wear loose clothing, such as neckties or shirts with loose sleeves, or jewelry, such as rings, necklaces or bracelets, when working on power equipment, and tie back long hair to prevent it from getting caught in your equipment. The author and editors who compiled this book have tried to make the contents as accurate and correct as possible. Plans, illustrations, photographs and text have been carefully checked. All instructions, plans and projects should be carefully read, studied and understood before beginning construction. Due to the variability of local conditions, construction materials, skill levels, etc., neither the author nor Popular Woodworking Books assumes any responsibility for any accidents, injuries, damages or other losses incurred resulting from the material presented in this book.

METRIC CONVERSION CHART

TO CONVERT	TO	MULTIPLY BY
Inches	Centimeters	2.54
Centimeters	Inches	0.4

Making Money Making Furniture. Copyright © 1999 by Blair Howard. Manufactured in the United States of America. All rights reserved. No part of this book may be reproduced in any form or by any electronic or mechanical means including information storage and retrieval systems without permission in writing from the publisher, except by a reviewer, who may quote brief passages in a review. Published by Popular Woodworking Books, an imprint of F&W Publications, Inc., 1507 Dana Avenue, Cincinnati, Ohio 45207. (800) 289-0963. First edition.

Visit our website at www.popularwoodworking.com for information on more resources for woodworkers.

03   02   01   00   99   5   4   3   2   1

Library of Congress Cataloging-in-Publication Data

Howard, Blair.
　　Making money making furniture / by Blair Howard.
　　　　p.　　cm.
　　Includes index.
　　ISBN 1-55870-500-7 (alk. paper)
　　1. Woodworking industries. 2. Woodwork. 3. Home-based businesses. I. Title.
HD9773.A2H69　1999
684.1'0068—dc21   99-17163
                                                                            CIP

Edited by R. Adam Blake
Production edited by Bob Beckstead
Cover designed by Angela Lennert Wilcox
Interior designed by Brian Roeth
Production coordinated by Kristen D. Heller
Technical drawings by Blair Howard
Icons © Digital Vision

THANKS

To Adam Blake, my editor, Bruce Stoker and all the other people at Popular Woodworking books who worked so hard to make this book work.

Thanks also to the good folks at Delta International Machinery, Porter Cable, Jesada Tools and American Clamping for their help and support.

ABOUT THE AUTHOR

Blair Howard's interest in woodworking began more than forty years ago in high school in England. His interest in furniture, especially antique furniture, goes back even farther. Apart from a short stint as a carpenter for a construction company, his woodworking was never more than a some-time hobby. Then, as a result of corporate downsizing, he suddenly found himself looking for work. So, the hobby became a source of income. Today, his work is much in demand and sells to all sorts of markets: galleries, furniture stores, factory outlets and to individuals. Blair, who is also the author of *Building Classic Antique Furniture With Pine* (Popular Woodworking books, 1998), resides in Cleveland, Tennessee.

table of contents

"What great things would you attempt if you knew you could not fail?" Those are not my words; they belong to Dr. Robert Schuller. Think about them. They hint of a whole new world of grand possibilities. I first heard them more than 15 years ago, and they've been a constant source of inspiration ever since. Those words forced me out of the rut and onto the highway, so to speak. Because of them I started to write—this is my fourteenth book. Later, they gave me my start in the business of woodworking. Today, those same words keep me motivated. Have they made me successful? Perhaps. Success is subjective: To some people it's making a great deal of money; to others it's the freedom to do as you please; to still others it might be something entirely different. Although I don't have great material wealth, I do make enough money to live quite comfortably, and I certainly have the freedom to do as I please. So, yes. Those words have made me successful. They can do the same for you. All you need is a little imagination, an idea and the will to win.

Can you make money making furniture? Of course. This book will show you how you can get started almost immediately, even as soon as next week, if you like. But this is not a "get rich quick" book. The information you'll find within these pages is the result of several years of trial and error—the years I spent turning a woodworking hobby into a serious source of income—a lot of help from a number of friends, and the benefits of my many years in sales and marketing.

WHAT THIS BOOK IS ABOUT

This book is not full of theory and wild ideas that may or may not work. It's a practical guide that offers real results, and quickly. You'll find no fluff here; no pie in the sky and no grand promises. You can take this information and make a good living, *starting tomorrow*. How can you be sure? Because this is exactly what I do, every day. The information has all been tried and tested in the field and today provides me with a good living, the freedom to come and go as I please and the ability to control my own future; something I never had when I was working for someone else.

PRACTICAL INFORMATION

Aside from providing you with all the information you need to make money making furniture, this book is unique because it takes the business process a step further. Other "how to make money" books provide only so much theory—some of it good, some no more than the product of a vivid imagination—and then they leave you high and dry to come up with a salable product on your own. You're then faced with months, perhaps even years, of hunting around for a product that will not only sell, but that is practical and easy to build. This book is different because the information you'll find here isn't theory. The techniques you are about to learn are those I've developed over the years doing exactly what the title of the book offers: *Making Money Making Furniture*.

BEST-SELLING PROJECTS

This book does something no other book in its class does: It provides you with the products that will make your efforts successful right away. It includes ten of my best-selling pieces, complete with working drawings, cutting lists and step-by-step instructions and photographs. These are my bread-and-butter pieces. They won't make you rich, but they will provide you with a good living and a base from which to grow your fledgling business. I also do something no one else will: I give you some realistic numbers to shoot for.

SMALL INVESTMENT— EASY TO SELL

You can begin with a very small investment; just the basic workshop tools, a minimal quantity of stock and a commitment to success. You'll find the marketing process easy to follow and implement. The projects, for the most part, are fairly simple to make and, as I have found from experience, even easier to sell.

AVOID MISTAKES

This book can and will enable you to turn your hobby into a source of extra money, or even a full-time business, almost instantly. It will also show you how to avoid

most of the mistakes that come from lack of experience. Over the years I've spent woodworking for a living, I've made all of those mistakes and more. Some were real doozies: expensive, to say the least. This book doesn't have all the answers, but it will show you how to avoid the mistakes I've made and many more of the traps and pitfalls you're bound to encounter doing business for yourself.

How often have you said to yourself, I wish I knew then what I know now? Well, this book offers just that opportunity: You can know now what has taken me many years to learn.

HOW THIS BOOK WORKS

Chapter one discusses the money you can make making furniture, both part time and full time, and such weighty considerations as overhead, tooling, work ethic and the places where you should or should not conduct your business.

Chapter two provides information on what sells and why, at least as far as the woodworker-turned-businessperson is concerned, and explains the advantages you have as an individual in a price-driven marketplace. You'll learn about your buyers' motives, your competition and how to establish a good reputation—and how to keep it.

Chapter three explains who your customers are and where to find them. It deals with each class of customer in depth, explaining what they like and why and how to deal with them. You'll learn how to sell directly to the public and thus make extra profits, and you'll discover the various wholesale outlets that can and will buy your products. These include galleries, factory outlets, fine furniture stores, interior designers and architects. You'll also learn how to work through craft shows, flea markets, country stores and craft shops.

Chapter four provides you with some basic sales skills: How to make your presentation, how to close the sale and how to answer objections. It also shows you how to build your portfolio of sales tools: samples, photographs, business cards and flyers.

Chapter five discusses the tools you'll need to make money making furniture: stationary power tools, portable power tools and nonpower tools.

Chapter six discusses the materials you'll use in your endeavors: types of wood, hardware, finishing materials and fasteners. It also offers advice on where and how to shop.

Chapter seven is about construction: joints, tools and the methods used to build

the pieces in the project section of the book.

Chapter eight is about finishing the product, which is perhaps the most important part of preparing a new piece of furniture for sale. A well-finished piece will always sell; a poorly finished piece probably never will. You'll learn how to produce a professional finish, how to fill grain and how to sand it smooth. Then the finishes themselves—stains, polyurethanes, combination finishes and shellac—are covered. Some of the pieces in the project section are painted; those finishes are covered too.

Chapter nine is about pricing your work. I've detailed the method I use. It's unconventional, but it works and is sure to provide a profit at a price that will be acceptable to buyers of all types.

Chapter ten introduces plans to make ten surefire best-sellers. These projects will provide you with an income almost instantly. They are tried and true, the products on my list of all-time top-ten best-sellers. And they still provide me with a major part of my income. Some of these projects, by themselves, can make you money. And that, after all, is exactly what this book is all about.

HOW MUCH CAN YOU MAKE?

Because this book is all about making money making furniture, it's logical to begin by taking a look at how much money you can realistically expect to make doing so. This chapter will give you at least an idea of how much money you can realistically expect to make working either part time or full time.

IMPORTANT QUESTIONS

Begin by asking yourself a couple of questions. The answers are very important, so think about them and take your time. Grab a notebook and a pencil and write your answers down. It's a process that will help you understand your own train of thought and help you to think clearly.

TAKE NOTES

The first question is: How much money do you *want* to make? That's a fairly simple question, isn't it? No, it isn't, and it's not even the right question. I *want* to earn a million dollars, which is possible but not realistic. The right question is twofold: How much money do you want to earn, and is it possible? The answers are entirely dependent on a number of related facts and situations: time, overhead, tooling, space, organization, location, the type of furniture you'll make, how much help

you can count on from family and friends, the degree of your own woodworking skills and the level of your commitment to that upon which you are about to embark. Take a moment to think about these issues and make notes.

Now, I know you're eager for numbers, so let's take an initial stab at the answer. We'll do this on two levels: working part time and working full time. First, I'll cover the basics, and then I'll go into detail.

THE NUMBERS—PART TIME

First let's assume you've decided you simply want to make some extra money for tools and equipment, and that you'll do it working nights and weekends. Because your livelihood will not depend on your efforts, your earnings will be proportionately lower than they would be if the reverse was true. Working nights and weekends, you should have no trouble earning $5,000 the first year (you'll learn how in a moment). That's not much, I hear you say. I say it's not bad. It's about $100 a week, and it's realistic.

THE NUMBERS—FULL TIME

Now let's assume you've decided to take the plunge and head out on your own; not exactly what I'd recommend, at least until

you have an idea of your limitations, but what the heck. How about $40,000 *net* the first year? The operative word here is *net*, and that assumes a gross closer to $80,000. Possible, but hardly likely; $25,000 is probably closer to what you can realistically expect. Again, you might say, that's not much. I say you're wrong. If you can take home $25,000 net your first year in business, especially working on your own, you'll have done better than nine out ten of those who've gone before. If you can do that, the future for you is boundless. Each year will be a little better than the one before and, if you decide to expand, employ some help and extend your market and your horizons, you could well be the next giant in the industry. But, for now at least, let's keep our feet on the ground.

HOW ABOUT HIRING SOME HELP?

Although this book is written for the individual who wants to make money making furniture, there are, of course, limits to how much one person can achieve working alone. But this book assumes that's exactly how you will begin. Someday, you might consider hiring some help, but that will bring a whole new set of problems: workers that lay out, government paperwork, health and Social Security benefits, the IRS, dealing with people who can't think for themselves and so on. Yes, I tried it, but not for long. After only a few short months I returned to solo status.

YOU'LL NEED TO SPECIALIZE

Whatever you do, you'll probably need to specialize, if only because familiarity leads to efficiency and, if you're working alone, efficiency leads to profit. The projects in this book offer a couple of possibilities. You can specialize in making small, easy and quick-to-build pieces and selling them to a broad market, or you can go with the big-ticket items and a small customer base. Having said that, in the interests of freedom and enjoyment, my specialties have developed and broadened over the years. Many of the pieces I make, I make many times over. But each time I do, rather than get into mass-production, I try to make each one unique. This allows me to be efficient and still maintain a high level of interest.

So, how did I arrive at the numbers? Let's do the part-time income first.

PART-TIME INCOME
Develop Your Skills

This book assumes you already have the basic woodworking skills necessary to build at least some, if not all, of the pieces described. And once you begin making furniture for money, those skills will develop. You'll find yourself working, automatically and without thought, through processes you once had to think through step by step. A piece that might take 20 hours to build today will eventually take no more than 5—once you've been at it for a while, that is.

Impact of Overhead and Other Considerations

If you're working part time in your garage your overhead will be small, so you don't have to worry about that too much. Your heat and light bills rise somewhat, of course, but most of your money will be spent on supplies: wood, glue, sanding materials and so on.

Space

Space is always a consideration but, once again, as we are talking about a part-time income, you won't need as much as you would if you were embarking on a new career. In fact, you'll find you can manage quite well in that single-bay garage. Even so, the more space you have, the better. A double-bay garage would provide a luxurious amount of space, and a custom-built shop 20′ by 20′ is the stuff of dreams.

Tooling

Tooling is important, even at the weekend level. You don't need much, but it should be the best you can afford: If you can't make an accurate cut, you can't make a salable piece of furniture. (You'll find this subject covered in depth in chapter five.) That brings us to the time element.

Time

The amount of money you'll make is directly proportional to the amount of time you spend actually making furniture. That doesn't mean time spent at work. You can

MISTAKE NUMBER 1: DON'T QUIT YOUR DAY JOB—YET

You've guessed it. The first mistake I made was the result of an overblown confidence in my own abilities and resources. Without much thought toward the future, I quit a well-paying job and plunged headlong into a world I really knew very little about. True, I'd been a sales manager for many years and knew all about how to sell a quality product—and I certainly was capable of building such a product—but I had little idea of what was involved when it came to replacing one good living with another. Yes, I had some savings. But they were soon eaten up by this, that and the other thing, leaving me eking out only a bare existence for more than a year. It was the unknown that hit me hard, and prematurely quitting my job was only the first in a long line of expensive mistakes I made during those early years, each one compounded by the one before. You, however, have an advantage I didn't have: this book. If only I knew then what I know now . . . Think hard before you make the leap into the void.

spend a whole day working hard and never hit a productive lick.

The $5,000 mentioned previously assumes you'll spend at least a couple of nights and most weekends hard at work. If you work six to eight hours a week actually producing pieces to sell, you'll earn about $12 to $14 an hour, *net*. Easy! But are you working only eight hours? No, because you have other things to do that will take at least that much time and probably more. There are customers to see, deliveries to make, trips to the hardware store, to the lumberyard, to the paint store, to the bank (hopefully) and so on. Then there's downtime when the table saw, or the radial arm saw, or even the electric drill motor is out of service. You can expect to spend at least one hour in nonpro-

ductive activity for every hour you spend actually producing.

FULL-TIME INCOME
Fun + Responsibility

Now, making furniture full time for a living is an entirely different story. Now the fun has to be tempered with responsibility. What once was no more than a pleasant, even lucrative, pastime has suddenly become the means by which you'll put bread on your table, feed your family and pay the bills. Your very existence will depend on the decisions you must make *before you begin*. Unless you have a little money set aside, you should think hard before you quit your job and embark on a wild ride into the unknown. It might be best to start out on a part-time basis, to build your skills, customer base, tooling and product line, and then take the proverbial plunge.

Longer Hours

Apart from your basic woodworking skills, the amount of time you dedicate to your new career is probably the most important aspect of turning your hobby into a business. There's no doubt that you'll be working long hours seven days a week, at least for the first couple of years. And, again, not all that time will be spent actually in the shop. Remember all that nonproductive activity, downtime and so on? You can expect all that and more. Now you'll also be dragged away to answer the telephone, often at the most inconvenient times. But you

have to do it: You never know what exciting new prospect might be on the other end of the line. True, an answering machine can cover the bases while you're away from the shop, but it can't close an important sale or handle an impatient potential customer—one that might not leave a message or call back. Then there's the extra paperwork to deal with, stocks of lumber to check, hardware, paint, stain, storage, etc. In fact, if you spend more than 60 percent of your time doing that which you love best, actually building the furniture, you'll be doing far better than most.

Overhead

There's your overhead to consider as well, especially your shop. Once again, don't jump in at the deep end. You'll be surprised just how much you can achieve working out of your garage. Yes, space is a major consideration, especially when you're working on several pieces at once. But if you have a two-car garage you can utilize during the early years, or even a small shop in your yard, you should be able to make do, at least for a while. Even after more than four years, I am still working out of a $16' \times 12'$ home-built shop in my yard and using my garage for storage, and I intend to continue that way for as long as I can. Space is at a premium, but so is cash.

Overhead

The following list of expenses is just a guideline. Depending on where you're located, you can expect to pay more or less.

RENT: $400–$1,000 or more per month

MORTGAGE (if you decide to buy): $750 and up per month for commercial property

TELEPHONE: $50 and up per month

ELECTRICITY, SEWER, WATER AND GAS: $250 and up per month

OFFICE SUPPLIES (BASIC): $50 per month

BUILDING MAINTENANCE: $100 per month (at least)

TRAVEL TO AND FROM YOUR SHOP: $50 per month

How About Tooling?

Tooling is important. To do the job right, you'll need the best. The "experts" say you can get by with only a few hand tools and a table saw. Bull! If you want to make a living, you have to be efficient and meet customer deadlines as well as your own. You have to have the basics first, and then you can add the equipment that's not essential but will broaden your scope and increase efficiency. And it all has to be good quality. The sweetness of low price is long forgotten when you have to replace a shoddy piece of equipment. Good tools are expensive, but you can build as you go. (I'll discuss tooling in depth in chapter five.)

You Really Do Need To Specialize

The type of furniture you'll build is also a major consideration, and will depend largely on your tooling and available

MISTAKE NUMBER 2: DON'T MOVE AWAY FROM HOME—YET

This one I didn't make. Don't rent a building you can't afford; it will eat you alive. Rent, which is what seems to interest people the most, is only a part of the outlay. Along with it you'll need to pay for electricity, water, telephone, maintenance and repairs, etc., etc. Work out of your home (as I *still* do) if you can, at least until you've built your business to the point where you can afford the extra expense. How do you know when you can afford to move? The answer is subjective, and will depend largely on how comfortable you feel with the size of your bank account. Only *you* will know when the time is right, if at all. My advice is this: If you can cope adequately with the amount of work you are producing in the space you already have, stay where you are. Those few extra feet of space can be an expensive luxury at best—and an alligator that will eat you alive at worst.

space. It's best to start out making some of the smaller pieces you'll find in the project section of this book, and then you can graduate to the larger items when you feel more comfortable with what you're doing.

Organization

You'll need to be organized: Your shop must be kept impeccably clean and tidy, and you must keep up with your orders, paperwork, stock and so on. Lack of organization will cost you time, which in turn will cost you money, more than you can imagine, and the cost won't even be obvious. For example, little things, like time spent looking for a simple router bit, pencil, pattern or measure, will take time away from production. Not much time by themselves, but put them all together and they add up: Over a year, the time and money you can lose is unbelievable. The old adage, a place for everything and everything in its place, can have a significant impact on your income.

DEDICATED OR DEAD?

You'll also need to make a commitment. Success is not an easy thing to achieve; ask any of the hundreds of thousands who start out in business each year and fail. That doesn't have to happen to you, and it won't if you follow the steps and procedures laid out in this book.

YOU HAVE THE ADVANTAGE

So, as you can see, the process of making money making furniture is quite involved, but it doesn't have to be intimidating. The system I've laid out for you will work. I know, because it worked for me—and still does. I have already broken the ground for you. The products detailed in the project section are all profitable to make, in de-

mand, easy to sell and will provide you with a nice income. Like food and clothing, furniture is one of the staples of life; it's a necessity. Everyone has to have chairs to sit on, a table to put food on, cupboards to store it in, beds to sleep on and so on. There's little you can make that will not sell sooner or later.

DON'T GIVE UP

Finally, there's this: Never give up. Quitters never win. Even when your problems seem to have grown to the point where they will overwhelm you, something *will* turn up; believe me. There was never a time in my life when this wasn't true. People say I'm lucky, and I suppose I am. But you know, the old adage is true: The harder I work, the luckier I get. Hang in there and work hard, not just at building furniture, but at building your business, and everything will work out in the end. I promise.

chapter two

KNOW WHAT SELLS AND WHY

People buy products for all sorts of reasons. Sometimes motives are hard to see, but there are two that are always a factor in the buying decision: price and quality. There are others of course—color, style, whim, decor, etc.—but price and quality will be a large part of the deal. And there's one other reason that's only slightly less important than the first two: the personality of the seller. I learned a long time ago that people only buy from people they like, and that applies to every section of the marketplace: retail or wholesale. If the buyer doesn't like you, she won't buy from you, and that's a fact.

WHAT SELLS AND WHY

Furniture is one of those products that always sells well. True, some items sell more quickly than others, but sooner or later, everything will go. There's no accounting for taste; you only need to look around any of the major furniture stores in your area to see that. For our purposes, though, we can break the product down into several distinct classes. There's the upscale fine furniture that only the rich can afford; there's the expensive stuff turned out by such outfits as Broyhill; there's the trendy pseudo-reproduction furniture made by such giants as Ethan Allen and Habersham Plantation;

there are oak furniture outlets where you can buy pieces made from real wood at fairly reasonable prices; and, finally, there are the low-price, mass-market furniture stores and outlets where everything seems to be made of pressed board and MDF. Each has a market of its own. Your problem is to find out what will work for you and how to sell it in a price-driven market place, quickly: You have to find a niche.

MAKE NEW FRIENDS

Personality is something you're born with, right? No, personalities are developed, and public relations will be a big part of what you do from now on. The sales manuals all say the customer is always right. Now we know that's not always true. But, in the interests of making a sale, you'd better believe that it almost always is. It's one thing to educate your buyer, but it's quite another to argue with him. You might win the battle, but you'll almost certainly lose the sale and gain a lot of bad publicity as well. Who knows how many people your customer will tell about his bad experience at your hands? And you can bet he will never tell the story from your point of view. Be nice. Be helpful. Be flexible. Be honest. Keep your promises. People only buy from people they like. What does this mean to you? Today, the buzz-

word is *networking*. The more friends you have, the larger your potential customer base, because people also talk about people they like in a positive way. The people who like you, your friends, will advertise you and your product in ways you can't even begin to imagine.

PRICE

Price is a complex word that doesn't always mean what you think it means. Often, price is confused with something else: cost. *Price* is what you pay for an item; *cost* is what happens when that product fails to perform as it should. For example, there has been much ado in the airline industry of late about the problem of counterfeit spare parts, and rightly so. Aircraft engine parts, even small ones such as nuts and bolts, are very expensive. For an original part, say a $3'' \times \frac{3}{8}''$ fine-thread bolt, the price might be as much as $12 or $15, but for a noncertified bolt the same size, the price would be much lower, say only a couple of dollars. The difference is that the certified bolt will hold up under extreme pressure; the cheaper version might not. If the cheaper version is installed the savings is perhaps $10; if the engine fails because of it, the *cost* could be incalculable.

Unfortunately, price is the strongest buying motive of all, and those in the furniture industry know this better than anyone else. You only have to listen to the ads constantly running on TV and on the radio, and read those in your local news-

papers, to understand what I mean. Day after day, week after week, we are bombarded by offers of 40 percent, 50 percent and even 60 percent off every item in the store; no down payment; no interest and no payments for up to three years. All this is price related, geared toward bringing in new customers and moving the product off the floor, seemingly without the use of money at all, at least for a while. And it works. Can you compete? Of course. Those store prices are not really low at all. Markup in the furniture industry is often 400 percent and more; a 50 percent discount still leaves the retailer with a profit often in excess of 100 percent.

QUALITY

Quality is always a consideration, but often only when the price is right. Most people think they're buying quality when they're not. The mass-market furniture industry goes to great lengths to disguise what is essentially garbage in its efforts to appeal to those looking for a high-quality product at the best price. They do this not only at the manufacturing stage, but in their advertising too. For instance, *real* cherry is quite different from *solid* cherry. Real cherry may be nothing more than MDF with an outer cladding of cherry veneer; solid cherry is exactly that. The old adage, if it seems to good to be true, it probably is, certainly applies to the furniture industry. Here's another saying that's just as true: The bitterness of poor quality will remain long after the sweetness of low price has gone.

So, as price and quality are both very important to both the furniture-buying public and trade, you will have a difficult time competing, right? Wrong. Now we come to the "why" part of this chapter.

PRICE AND QUALITY

Believe it or not, you can provide both price and quality, and a lot more besides. The advantages you, as a small, independent manufacturer, have over the great mass-production factories are manyfold.

1. You can supply a quality piece made from solid wood at a very attractive price.

2. You can supply custom-built furniture (something very few large manufacturers or furniture stores can do), also at attractive prices.

3. You can provide furniture in a variety of finishes to order.

4. You can fill small orders to the trade quickly—one piece of this, two of that—where ordinarily they would have to wait up to six months for such deliveries.

5. You can sell top-quality products made of solid wood directly to the public at prices that compete favorably with the low-priced MDF junk found in many of the larger chains and department stores. In fact, once the word gets around, you'll find you have more work than you can handle—if you can keep your promises, that is.

6. You can make money. Good money. That's all well and good but, as you can

TRUE STORY

One day I stumbled on a small country store that specialized in handmade, country-style furniture. I wandered around for a long time, looking and making mental notes, surprised at the poor quality of the product. Then I approached the owner and we chatted for a while. I picked her brain. I wanted to know just what sold and what didn't. Finally, I told her what I trying to do and asked if she'd be interested in taking a look at what I might have to offer. She agreed. I even noticed a gleam in her eye, but never considered for a minute what it might mean. Anyway, I left her store that day with a list of her most popular items— the fast movers—and promise that if she liked my work she'd try a piece or two.

I spent a couple of days making one or two of the smaller items, and then I returned. You should know that at this stage I had no idea what to charge for the things I'd made. But she was a nice lady, and I felt sure we could come to an arrangement we could both be happy with. I was wrong. I soon understood the significance of that strange gleam in her eye: This woman was all business, and she knew exactly how to handle the likes of me. Yes, she liked what I had to offer, but only at a price she dictated. Oh, she was good. I not only left her store with less money than I'd anticipated, I now had an order for more of the same; it wasn't long before I realized that at this rate I could go broke: Well, starve, maybe. So what was I to do? This nice but tough woman was willing to give me the start in the business I'd been looking for, but only on her terms.

I now was faced with two choices: I could continue with her, get my feet wet if you like, or I could drop her and try a new approach. Now, I've always been a believer in the old saying, a bird in the hand is worth two in the bush, so I decided to stick with her. It was a decision I've never regretted. Through her I was able to build a portfolio of sales tools, hone my skills, learn more than a little about the business and build something of a reputation. And then: Guess what. As my work became more and more in demand, I was able to raise my prices, and she was able to raise hers too. Not only was I now making good money on the furniture she bought, but her profits jumped as well, and she was one happy store owner. More than that, I was able to start my list of hot-selling products. No, they didn't all come from that experience, just a few in fact, but those that did were the base for what was to come next. Today, that first customer is still one of my best, and good friend too.

imagine, furniture can be a notoriously slow-moving product. Take a look at the large stocks held by the big chains and independents, and you'll see what I mean.

SO, WHAT SELLS?

There are certain pieces that everyone seems to want or need. These are the pieces from which you'll build your product line. They sell well because everyone has to have them, in one form or another. It took me a long time to find the products described in the project section. I started out, as most people do, with an idea and little else. I knew I could make salable furniture, but I didn't know what to make. At first, I thought a nice piece, whatever it was, would sell easily and quickly. Not so. In fact, I spent many months of trial and error before I found even one piece that would generate repeat sales. I wandered around the furniture stores, asked questions and made notes, all to little or no avail; I wasn't yet at the stage where I felt comfortable approaching a corporate buyer, or even an independent store owner.

TEN TOP MOVERS

The ten products included in this book represent the bread and butter of my business. All have sold consistently over the years and continue to do so. If you never try anything else, you can make a good living from them alone. I have sold more than 100 of the veggie bins, just as many of the over-commode

cabinets, almost as many of the sofa tables, dozens of blanket chests, several dozen jelly cabinets and bookcases, 38 entertainment centers of one sort or another, a couple dozen computer desks and more shelves than I could count. Yes, I make other products. Most of them are special orders, but once I add them to my portfolio, they repeat again and again. Some are large, complicated pieces; some are small and easy to make. They are all made possible only because of my top ten and a few others that sell equally well.

SOMETHING TO BUILD ON

Lay the foundation of your business with these ten products, and then take a look around the furniture shops, ask questions, go to the library and borrow some books. When you have time to play, to create, you can begin to build a portfolio of your own. By the way, it's essential that you do set aside time to play—to create new products. After all, woodworking is fun.

YOUR REPUTATION IS YOUR INCOME

Finally, remember that while price is important to your customers, most will expect a high-quality product no matter what you charge. You can't get away with shoddy workmanship and cheap materials simply because your price is low. Try it, and it will cost you dearly. A reputation is a terrible thing to lose. Even in a large city, word soon gets around; in a small town, bad publicity will quickly drive you out of business.

chapter three

FINDING YOUR CUSTOMERS

If you are going to make money making furniture, you'll need an outlet for your work. That's a simple statement, and an even simpler concept. But the process of finding customers is not simple at all, especially when you have no idea of where or how to begin. Not so, you might say. I can start by selling to my family and friends and move on from there. Absolutely not. Sell to the people you know and love best, and you'll alienate your family members and probably lose your friends.

YOUR MARKET

Your customers will be drawn from a very large pool consisting of the general public at large—retail—and a variety of trade outlets that range from low end to high end, with a whole range of possibilities in between. At the high end will be fine furniture stores and galleries; at the low end the mass-market outlets where cheap and shoddy are the bywords. In between you'll have craft shows, craft shops, country stores (yes, there's a difference), oak furniture outlets, architects, interior designers, schools, churches, garden centers, office supply houses and even hotels. All these, and more, are ready outlets for the small, independent furniture maker.

MISTAKE NUMBER 3: KEEP IT OUT OF THE FAMILY

This is a mistake I made only once, but it was a bad one. A fairly close member of my family asked how much it would cost to make a kitchen island—a freestanding cupboard with a butcher-block top. At first I wasn't sure what to say, if anything. But then I thought, a sale is a sale. I'll do her a favor. I'll let her have it at cost. So I did the math in my head and gave her a price. She wrinkled her nose, and then nodded her head and said OK. Well, to cut a long story short, I'd underestimated the cost—never work prices out in your head; the butcher block alone was worth the price of the piece—and I wasn't at all happy, but I didn't increase my price. Worse was yet to come. She took the piece without complaint, but has since let it be known—though not to me— that I'd overcharged her for the thing, and that she'd never trust me again. It turns out that she'd expected me to make the piece for her for free. *Never work for family and friends. You can't win and, especially where family is concerned, they never go away.*

DIRECT SELL OR WHOLESALE?

Your problem is to find out what type of outlet will work best for you and how to sell to it in a price-driven marketplace, quickly: You have to find a niche. Will you sell direct to the public and thus command a higher price? Or will you sell to retail stores, galleries and outlets? Sell direct and you'll make more money on each piece you move, true. But that can create problems you won't encounter if you sell direct to the trade. You won't have to deal with finicky, picky customers. You won't have to advertise to reach your prospective customers. Delivery time will cut by up to 80 percent because you'll drop off several pieces at one location during daylight hours instead of having to run all over the area to deliver at all hours of the day and night. I do sell some pieces direct to the public, but most go out to the trade. It was a decision I made early on in my business career. Yes, the extra money you'll make from a direct sale is nice, but the professional treatment you'll receive at the hands of the trade is well worth the cut in price.

DIRECT SELL—RETAIL

There are many ways you can reach out to the general public (retail): advertising, renting space on the floor of your local mall, renting space at a flea market or simply putting your wares on show under a temporary shelter on the side of the road in a rest area. Advertising is a subject unto itself, and is discussed, at least as it applies to the small businessperson on page 27. Space in your local mall—those displays they often have in the open areas—can be expensive, but will expose you to large numbers of potential buyers. If you're interested, contact the mall marketing office for rates and availability. Flea markets are discussed in detail later in this chapter. As to setting up in a rest area, I've seen it done, but wouldn't recommend it. Who knows what might arrive in the next vehicle: It's not worth the risk.

CRAFT SHOWS

One of the best ways to reach the public at large is to rent space at a craft show. The only problem is you'll have to tailor your wares to suit your audience. People who attend these shows aren't looking for fine furniture. They are looking for country-style furniture, preferably inexpensive—which doesn't necessarily mean poor quality, although the workmanship of

MISTAKE NUMBER 4: DON'T PUT ALL YOUR EGGS IN ONE BASKET

This is one of the biggest mistakes you can make. Find a strong buyer and become involved with that buyer to the exclusion of all others, and you have a formula for disaster. Over a long and growing relationship with a single outlet, your investment in equipment, lumber and hardware will increase as your business grows. You may take out a loan, even hire extra hands to meet the demand for your products. Even your own personal income will come to depend upon this single outlet: Not a good idea. Suppose the unthinkable happens and you lose your only account. How will you maintain your income, especially in the short term? How will you pay your labor? How will you make payments on your loan?

This is not such an outlandish proposition as you might think. Businesses are bought out daily, and you might not get along so well with the new owner. Businesses go bankrupt, they burn, owners die—anything can happen, even a tornado. If the unthinkable happens you will be way out on a limb and suddenly without any income at all. Think about it. Such a disaster could mean the end of your business. At the very least, you'd have to start all over again.

Build a Bigger Basket

Your customer base should be at least a half-dozen strong and fairly diverse: a couple of oak factory outlets, a couple of country stores, a fine furniture store, a gallery and so on. Thus, if one account fails it won't bring your house of cards crashing down around your ears. Whenever you lose a customer, go out immediately and find a new one to replace it. Always maintain your base.

much of what you'll find at these shows leaves a lot to be desired, and prices do reflect that. Besides offering a ready market and a somewhat captive audience for your work, there are many other benefits to attending craft shows. For instance, you'll learn more about making money making furniture faster than in any other sales environment.

A Learning Environment

First, you'll learn from your peers, especially from those that have spent a lifetime attending such shows. These are the veterans of their world. They know all the wrinkles. Better yet, they are willing to talk about it. There is a camaraderie within the craft show community, and the members are always ready to welcome a newcomer. Within minutes of erecting your shelter, and even before, you'll have a steady stream of visitors, most of them offering help or advice. Don't be proud: Be outgoing and ready to listen. These are the people who will teach you the trade.

Move Out and Mingle

During quiet periods, take off and visit other vendors. Let them know who you are. Hand out your card (see chapter four). Make new friends. Ask questions and listen to the answers. Take note of what your competitors are stocking; if they've been at it for a while, it's what they are selling. These people don't waste time and effort loading and unloading, carting

CRAFT SHOWS CAN BE A WAY OF LIFE

Some people begin going to craft shows simply because they don't know where else to start. Many of them never move on. They find something there that's appealing far beyond the money they inevitably seem to make. I mentioned that there's a camaraderie among crafters, and I'm sure that's why many of them live out their lives on the road, moving from one show to the next and returning home only to build replacements. The friend that got me started in the furniture business is one of these people. He's in his late sixties now. His wife suffers from Alzheimer's, but she still attends all the shows. From May until Christmas, every weekend, you'll find his old white van parked at the rear of the pitch. Some weekends are good, and he'll sell a couple of thousand dollars worth of stock; some are not so good, and he might do little more than make his expenses. No matter. The shows are not only his way of life, they are his life. After more than 25 years, this old man has more friends on the craft show circuit than you could possibly count, crafters and customers alike.

stuff this way and that and handling stock they know they're not going to sell. This you'll learn mostly from experience, but your new colleagues will surely give you some pointers.

You'll learn more faster from your customers and fellow crafters (they are always called *crafters*, no matter what they are selling) than you will in any other environment. Your peers will offer advice, whether you want it or not. The public at large will also be quick to point out that your work is expensive—especially if it is.

Researching Shows

How do you begin? First, go to the bookstore and buy a magazine. There are more than a dozen publications dedicated just to crafts and crafting. Inside you'll find ad-

vertisements for craft shows, mostly large events. Some will be "juried" shows. The chances are you won't be able to work one of these, at least in the beginning. To qualify, your product must fit the general theme of the juried show, and the quality of your work must pass inspection by the selection committee—the jury. Open shows where anyone can buy space if it's available are the ones you're looking for. Pick one that's not too far away and attend. It will most likely be held over a weekend. Take a hotel room and be there the day before the event opens to the public. Most shows allow vendors in on the afternoon before opening to set up. You should turn up too. Tell them at the gate that you intend to start attending craft shows and that you're looking for information and pointers. They'll be only too pleased to let you wander around and gossip. While you're there, ask a fellow crafter for an event calendar, which will list all future shows in the local area, and some far beyond, for the rest of the year. It will also provide a list of important addresses and phone numbers: the local association, officials and the like. These will be invaluable when you are ready to start attending for real. Above all, you're there to learn. Over the next 2 days you'll spend some 16 hours at the show, watching the public, observing the crafters and taking note of stock, prices, finishes, workmanship, presentation, etc. You should leave that first show a far wiser person than you were when you arrived.

Working A Show

Next, pick the show where you'll make your debut. It doesn't matter how large or small the show may be, although you're likely to sell more at a larger show, because this is to be another learning experience. But do give yourself some time to prepare, at least a couple of months.

Now you'll have some decisions to make. The first, and most important, is how much space you'll take. Start out small. Space, even at craft shows, is expensive. A single space—and some crafters take as many as four at a time—will, depending on the show, cost anywhere from $25 to $200 for the weekend. So start small and learn from the experience. A single space will allow you to exhibit quite a range of stock, from small pieces to large. Having made your decision, make the phone call to request an entry form. Fill it out and send it back with the fee enclosed as soon as possible. Space is always at a premium, and if you waste time you may not get in.

A Home of Your Own

Next, decide how you'll present your goods and, if it's an outdoor event, how to protect them from the elements. You can go to great expense and buy a custom-made, weatherproof canopy, or you can build your own. If you're attending only indoor shows this won't be a consideration. However, attend only indoor shows and you'll miss the best part of the experience. Outdoor shows are much more fun, even in bad weather.

Build It Yourself

If you decide to build your own canopy, you can do so quite inexpensively using ¾″ galvanized pipe and pipe fittings—elbows, junctions and splices—and blue waterproof tarp you can buy from any of a number of mail-order outlets or cut-price stores. The tarps will cost about $50; the pipe perhaps $100. Plan the structure carefully—something on the order of 12′ long by 8′ wide by 6½′ high should do quite nicely—and then buy your pipe cut to length and threaded at both ends. Then it's simply a matter of screwing all the pieces together and covering the structure with the tarps, which you'll tie tightly to the frame; you'll need an extra tarp to cover the front in case of rain. You'll also need some iron tent pegs to hold the tarp down. These you can make yourself from angle iron. Take a piece of ¾″ stock, grind one end to a point, split the other end about 2″ down the corner, and then bend the two flats back to form a hook that will hold the cords.

Taking It on the Road

Next you'll need some way of transporting your wares to market. If you have a minivan with removable back seats, this will do fine. If you have a pickup truck, that will work as well. But these small vehicles will not carry all your stock, so you'll have to make two (if not three) trips, at least on the outbound leg; hopefully you'll sell most of your stock and require only one trip to transport the remainder home. If you don't have a towhook on your van or truck, invest in having one fitted. Now you can rent one of those small U-Haul trailers. These are more than adequate to transport what you'll need to fill your single display space. When you've learned the ropes and are taking more space, you can either buy a panel truck or rent ever-increasing larger vans.

Smaller Is Better—At First

Once you have your booth and your transport, you'll need stock to fill it with. Almost all of the pieces described in the back half of this book will work. In the early days, though, when you're learning, it's a good idea to take only the smaller pieces. These are easy to build, transport and handle. They will also be priced at the low end of the range, and thus are perfect for impulse buyers (more about them later). The perfect items for a first-time exhibitor to stock would be an assortment of shelves, a dozen veggie bins, the same number of over-commode cabinets and a dozen blanket chests of varying sizes: somewhere between $3,000 and $4,000 worth of stock. These items are always in high demand at craft shows and, at a well-attended event, you should have little trouble selling out. Later, you can take larger, more ambitious pieces. But these will not move as fast as the smaller pieces.

More Essentials

As well as your stock, you'll need to take along several other items: a receipt book, something in which to keep your money, price tags, a couple of small folding tables on which to display smaller items such as the shelves, a portfolio of photographs (if you have one), pen or pencil, a notepad, a calculator and some business cards; I've never attended a craft show where I didn't get at least a couple of custom orders, often as many as ten (or even more). At this stage in the game, don't bother with credit card equipment; this may be your first and last craft show. Finally, there's the piper we all have to pay: the tax man. Yes, you'll be expected to collect and pay sales taxes even here at the craft show. Inspectors regularly patrol these supposedly unregulated retail outlets, and they will want to see your records. So charge your customers the appropriate amount of tax, keep your receipt book handy and expect a visit from the "Man."

Hurry Up and Wait

Once you're at the show, your tent is pitched and your stock is displayed for all to see, all you have to do is wait for the customers to arrive. Don't expect too much. The first show is always a learning experience, and should be regarded as such. It will also be a telling experience. Craft shows may not be for you. Some people love them, and others hate them; there seems to be little ground in between. Your first show may be your last, and that's OK. There are lots more outlets for your furniture if that turns out to be the case. For now, however, make the most out of the experience.

The Hidden Potential

People who attend craft shows are a friendly lot. They'll stop by, look at your goods and talk, and talk and talk. Many of them will be crafters themselves, and they'll want to know all about what you do, how you do it and why. Don't be afraid to get involved; that's how you'll learn. Many will be just lookers, having no intention of buying. Often, however, these peo-

---

MISTAKE NUMBER 4: DON'T WORK FOR NOTHING

Only once did I take an order for a custom-built piece of furniture and not take a deposit. *Custom-built* was the word. It was an entertainment center. One of those odd-shaped, odd-sized pieces, all shelves, with odd doors here and there. Together, we put the thing down on paper and I priced it. He liked what I'd suggested *and even offered a deposit*, which, of course, I turned down, saying something to the effect that I trusted him and a deposit wasn't necessary. Boy, was I wrong: The guy hadn't checked with his wife, and I got stuck with the piece. As it was made to fit the *gentleman's*—and I use that word advisedly—living room wall, it was of little use to anyone else, even at a discount. I ended up dismantling the piece; not a grand experience. *Always* take a deposit big enough to cover the cost of labor and materials.

ple buy on impulse. They see something they like and take it home with them. In fact, very few of the people who attend craft shows have any preconceived intention of spending more than a few dollars. So make conversation. When someone shows interest, ask questions; above all, listen to the answers. Take orders. When I used to attend shows, I did more business taking orders for custom pieces than I did selling the stuff I had on hand. Make sure you price your orders so that you'll make a profit. Obvious? Yes, but it's easy to underprice when you're involved in a sale. A word of warning: If you take an order for a custom-built piece, take a deposit too—at least 30 percent, and 50 percent if you can.

Finally

Depending on the quality of your goods, their customer appeal (hot items everyone needs) and how they're priced, you can expect an average show to yield between three or four hundred to several thousand dollars in sales; some shows are good, some are bad. Sales volume depends on many things, not the least of which is the weather. If you've taken the trouble to exhibit, give it a fair chance. Unless you really don't like the environment, in which case there's little point in doing it again, don't let low sales volume the first go-round put you off. On the other hand, there's no doubt a good first show and a couple of thousand dollars in sales will do

wonders for your attitude and your opinion of the venue.

ADVERTISING

Advertising is perhaps the most obvious way to reach out and sell someone. But it's not easy. Advertising is an art and a profession unto itself. People go to school for many years to learn its ins and outs. You can spend a lot of money on advertising for little or no return. It's best to stay away from the obvious: newspapers, magazines, radio and TV. And that would seem to be just about everything. Not true. There are lots of simple, inexpensive ways to get the word out, not the least of which is word of mouth. But that's putting the cart before the horse. It's difficult for people to recommend something they don't know about, and until you've sold your first piece, no one will know about your work; it's a catch-22 situation. So, for now, you'll have to come up with other ideas; here are some of mine.

The Local Weekly

I don't know about your town, but mine has a weekly tabloid filled with consumer ads: It's called *The Trader*. Almost every town has one; large cities have several. You'll find them for sale in supermarkets, gas stations and the like. Ours costs 75 cents, advertises everything from used diapers to trucks and has a large circulation. Best of all, it costs nothing to take out an ad. If you have one of these little papers

in your area, take out a small ad and run it every week. You don't need to say much. Don't get into specifics. Something like this will do nicely: *For sale: custom-built furniture—oak, pine, maple, etc. Reasonable prices. Call for details and quotes.* Put it in, let it run and forget it. You'll probably get little response for the first week or so. Don't get discouraged. If it runs long enough, curiosity will prevail. Soon you'll be getting a steady stream of calls, eight or ten a week, and that's all you need. If you can convert two or three of those calls into orders, you'll have more work than you can handle.

Handbills

If you don't have a *Trader*, you might try a small flyer. You can build one on your computer, or you can have the local quick-print build one for you quite inexpensively: Put it on bright-colored paper so it will attract attention. Again, you don't have to say too much. The same wording as the ad described above will do. Now pin the thing up on all the local bulletin boards you can find: in churches, supermarkets, public places, etc. You'll be surprised at the attention it gets. Once again, don't expect too much too soon.

Newspapers Are Not a Good Idea

Newspapers are one of the most expensive ways to advertise. Stay away from them. Think about it: How often do *you* read the display ads? Only the full- and half-page ads grab any real attention, and these are inordinately expensive. The small display ads are a complete waste of time: I know, I've tried them. The classifieds will bring in business, eventually, but they are expensive and offer little or no return for at least several weeks. No, newspaper advertising is not a good idea. Even at the local level you'll be competing with the mass-market furniture chains and their large display ads. Go that route and you'll soon become discouraged, wondering if you're even doing the right thing by trying to make money making furniture.

DIRECT SELLING

If you're lucky enough to have a place where you can display your wares—a workshop with road frontage or a home on the roadside in the country—you have an advantage you can't put a price on. Put one or two pieces of your furniture on show to passersby and you have an instant source of income. A small sign and a few well-chosen products will bring a steady stream of buyers to your door. You may never sell those display pieces, but the orders they bring will make them worth their weight in gold. Even the smallest storage area in your workshop can be made productive: Keep it clean and place your products so they can easily be seen, and you have your own gallery right there in your shop.

CRAFT SHOPS AND COUNTRY STORES

I've already discussed craft shops and country stores to some extent, but these little outlets can be pure gold—if you don't mind operating on their level. And by that I mean the furniture you'll sell here will be somewhat less expensive and certainly primitive. This is not to say that you can sacrifice quality; you can't. True, the majority of the goods you'll find in these places will be poor-quality pieces, but that's no reason for *you* to get down and dirty. This is your chance to build a solid client base. The trick is to maintain the primitive look while building in solid craftsmanship and quality.

Don't Sacrifice Quality

Most of the goods you'll find on sale in craft shops and country stores are literally thrown together: Boards are rough-sawn, little or no sanding is ever done, the finish is rarely more than a coat of stain, strong joints are nonexistent and construction is accomplished with a nail gun or drywall screws and so on. Thus, the product is almost always priced inexpensively, and that's an obstacle you'll have to overcome. In the early days, to get your foot in the door, you may have to match those prices—or near enough. Whatever you do, don't sacrifice quality for low prices. You can make high-quality country products using all of the best construction techniques, finish them properly and maintain the overall country expression, all without sacrificing quality. True, it will take you a little longer and thus cost a little more up front, but it's all fairly simple stuff, and the extra time and effort will pay off a hundredfold in the long run.

When your stuff stands side by side with that of your poor-quality competitors, the contest will be over. I know. I've been there.

Where To Find Craft Shops and Country Stores

The best place to begin, obviously, is in the yellow pages, although many owners may not bother to advertise this way. But through the yellow pages you should be able to make your first contacts. Look under "Crafts."

Ask questions and listen to the answers. One good contact will inevitably lead to another, and so on.

Attend local craft shows. Many country-store owners take space at these high-profile outlets, and they'll have time to talk.

Finally, as you drive around new areas or nearby towns, keep your eyes open. There seems to be one of these little outlets around almost every corner, and many don't bother to advertise, even in the yellow pages. This is especially so in the southeast. I've found several new customers this way.

Breaking the Ice

First, leave your portfolio and sales kit in the car: You don't want to look like a salesman. Go inside. Take time to look around; discover exactly what type of goods your prospect is selling. When you feel comfortable, ask to see the owner. Introduce yourself, compliment the owner on the store, explain what you do and then ask where they buy their stock. Listen carefully to the answer. You'll find most country-store owners are receptive to new sources. Crafters can be very limited in scope, and store owners are always looking for something new or something different.

Start Selling Right Away

Ask if the owner can spare a few moments to look at your book/portfolio of photographs (more about this later). If he agrees, take him through it slowly. Don't let him take it from you and flip the pages: Stay in control of the book. Don't talk too much. Instead, ask open-ended questions such as "What do you think of this piece?" This type of question will encourage conversation. If he indicates that he likes a particular piece, try to close the sale. Ask if he'd like to try one. If it's a small piece, ask if he'd like to try a half dozen.

FLEA MARKETS

Flea markets are another potential source of income, and they may fit well into your scheme of things, at least at the beginning of your business adventures. Flea markets come in various shapes and sizes. Stay away from the very small roadside versions. The best are those large affairs

fondly known as *flea market malls*. Many of the larger varieties are open seven days a week. Most, however, open only over the weekend, and that's why they suit woodworkers so well. You can work during the week building new stock and filling special orders from the week before, and then load it all up, set up shop in the flea market, sell most of it over the weekend and take more orders—and then repeat the process the following week. Neat. Best of all, large flea markets attract customers by the thousands, which means exposure on a grand scale.

What Does It Cost?

For what they offer, flea markets can be a very inexpensive way of doing business. Typically, a single space— $20' \times 12'$—depending on the location and popularity of the venue, will rent for anywhere from $25 to $75 per day with a 2-day minimum, and you'll be expected to sign a lease for at least three months, and perhaps as long as six months. The rent, however, includes your heat and light, which makes it very attractive; you will be expected to provide your own table and chairs, but in some instances you can even rent those too.

What to Stock and Show

Unless you're willing and financially able to take a large or double space, you won't be able to display a full range of products. This makes the choice of which items to include in your display very important. Each piece must earn its place in your limited display area; it must be able to attract attention. The small pieces described in the project section lend themselves well to the flea market atmosphere—the large pieces take up too much room. In addition, quilt racks, small chairs and tables, small bookcases, cupboards, bathroom-wall cabinets, candleholders, shelves of every shape and size, veggie bins, trash boxes, plate racks and so on are the type of things the typical flea market browser is looking for and will also work well. For the rest you'll have to rely on your portfolio, which should be prominently displayed up front for all to see.

Pricing for Flea Markets

Prices will necessarily be somewhat lower than you can command by selling direct. This, however, shouldn't be a problem. The loss will be more than made up for by the larger quantity you're bound to move. People who attend flea markets are looking for a bargain. Be sure you can provide one; if not, you'll soon gain a reputation for being expensive. Quality will not get you out of trouble here: Your customers expect both quality *and* a lower price. Prices, then, must reflect the venue, and for flea markets should be set some 15 percent to 20 percent lower than retail, but significantly higher than wholesale.

On the other hand, you'll be taking orders for custom work. The prices for these

pieces will reflect the unusual nature of the work and will be set somewhat higher than retail, perhaps by as much as 20 percent, but don't be greedy: Your customer will still be expecting a bargain.

The Upside of Flea Market Trading

- Low rent for your space
- Heat and light are provided—low overhead
- Large customer base of ready buyers
- You can your keep your space stocked with attractive, but inexpensive, quick-and-easy pieces: crowd pleasers
- You can solicit special orders for custom-built work (These will command a much higher price than your regular stock, from 20 percent to 50 percent more.)

The Downside of Flea Market Trading

- The retail price you can demand for your work will be lower than you can get by selling direct
- You may only have the weekend to open for business, which means you, and perhaps your spouse too, will be working seven days a week

OAK FURNITURE OUTLETS

These offer, perhaps, the best of opportunities for a budding entrepreneur looking to make money making furniture. Most are small, independently owned and most are incredibly successful. They operate on a much smaller markup than regular furniture stores, and thus are very interested in finding low-cost sources. This is where you come in. But you have much more to offer the outlet type of business than just a lower price.

Why Should They Buy From You?

• Low Price: Every buyer is looking to pay as little for his stock as he can. If you can supply a quality product at an attractive price, your foot will be well and truly in the door.

• Small quantities: Most large manufacturers require their customers to buy minimum orders, often as much as a truckload. You will be able to supply your outlets on a much smaller scale; thus your prospect's investment will be much smaller and will allow him to purchase more often and more discriminately.

• Quick turnaround: Typically, it takes a furniture manufacturer several months to fulfill an order. Just the fact that you can supply a quality product in two or three weeks will grab the buyer's attention. The ability to turn product into money quickly is one of the secrets of a successful retail business.

• Custom sizes and orders: Very few large manufacturers will even consider making one-off, custom-built pieces. This can and should be your stock in trade. There's never a day goes by that my outlets don't ask for something off the wall, an odd-sized version of an entertainment center, desk, sideboard, table and so on. These custom-built pieces command higher prices, and thus are more profitable to you and your outlet. This feature of your service will also open doors for you. You can build your business on these orders alone.

Quality

As always, quality is king. Even though most of the stock you see in a typical oak furniture outlet is not what you might call the best quality, your buyer will expect better from you. From his regular supplier he has to put up with what comes along the pipeline. Buying from you, however, offers him something different, something he can enjoy: personal, one-on-one contact with a supplier—and he will milk it for all it's worth. Not only will he expect better from you, he might even take some of his

---

MISTAKE NUMBER 5: DON'T BEAT THE PRICE JUST TO GET THE BUSINESS

The worst thing you can do, the biggest mistake you can make, is to beat a competitor's price simply to get the business. To take a loss on a product simply to get the order is to take the first step toward disaster. If you can't make a profit, it's best not to work at all. Too many losing projects will quickly put you into bankruptcy. If you know you can't meet a price, turn it down, firmly. Your prospect will respect you for it and will quickly get the idea that you know what you're doing and that you can't be intimidated; you'll build loyalty and respect. All these are a part of a productive, ongoing business relationship.

frustrations with other suppliers out on you. Don't be discouraged: It's not personal. He's just blowing off steam. Build a strong relationship with your outlet's buyer and supply a consistently good-quality product, and he will increasingly turn to you for what he needs.

Pricing

As always, pricing is something of an art, especially where these small independent oak furniture outlets are concerned. As an independent yourself, you will be expected to offer prices competitive with other suppliers, except where custom pieces are concerned. How is it done?

Ask And Ye Shall Be Given

In almost every case I ask what a buyer is paying now. That's not to say I always get an answer, or that the answer I do get is truthful, but whatever the answer, I do establish a starting point. I may not be able to match what he's paying, but slowly I build a picture of my customer's buying habits—and of my competitors' pricing structures. Yes, I always take notes.

Stick to Your Formula

If all else fails, stick to your own pricing formula. Establish a price you can live with and can be sure will make you a profit, and then stick to it.

MISTAKE NUMBER 6: DON'T BREAK YOUR WORD

If you gave a buyer a price, stick to it. If you make a mistake in pricing, it's your fault and not the buyer's. You'll have to eat the loss, at least on this delivery. What you do is explain the problem and assure your buyer that you intend to hold the price you gave him, but that you won't be able to repeat the sale without an increase. Your buyer will understand; we all make mistakes. Some will offer to cover your mistake and meet your new price now. The temptation to accept will be strong, but you should refuse, for a couple of reasons. First, and most important, your integrity is at stake, and the fact that you intend to keep your word, even if it means taking a loss, will impress your client and go a long way toward establishing trust and a lasting relationship. Second, a situation such as this can be a great selling opportunity. Often a customer placed in this position will want to do something to help ease your pain and will place another order, or an even larger order than normal. It's happened to me several times.

The Approach

You'll need your business card, portfolio of photographs and a sample targeted *specifically* to the oak factory type of outlet. That means you'll need to do a little research. Visit the store a couple of weeks before you make your sales visit. Take a look around. Find something nice, small and fairly easy to build. Get the price: You're sure to find it on a label but, if not, ask. Take measurements, and then go home and build the piece. Use only the best materials and make it the best job you've ever done, both in workmanship and finish. Which prompts me to mention a mistake many a would-be woodworker entrepreneur makes: Don't make the sample better than the product you'll make for sale (see the sidebar Mistake Number 7).

If you can't find something you like, build a country bookcase (Best-Selling Project 6): It's an attractive piece, your prospective customer won't have seen one before, and it's a fast seller. It's been my most successful door-opener for a long time. Often you'll receive an opening order for two, or even three: one golden oak, one Provincial and one dark oak.

Now you have your sample, you're ready to go. If you can, make an appointment to see the owner. When you arrive, leave your sample in your vehicle: Take in only your card and portfolio of photographs. Once inside, introduce yourself and quickly explain what you do. Now start selling. (Be sure to study the sales techniques in chapter four.)

Consignments?

Oak factory outlets like consignments; I don't, and neither should you. If you don't know what *consignment* means, let me explain. Your customer places an order for pieces he thinks he can sell; you supply the order, but you'll receive money only when a pieces sells and your outlet gets paid for it. Don't get involved. It might take several months to move even a single piece. In the meantime, you're out all your time and costs, with no real idea when you might get paid. In the early days you might be tempted to try it, just to establish yourself with a new client. Don't. Once you start this unprofitable way of doing business, you'll be expected to continue. No established manufacturer works on consignment, and neither should you.

GALLERIES

Galleries represent something different for the woodworker. They are not, perhaps, the first prospect that comes to mind when considering a list of potential customers. They do, however, represent a very lucrative outlet, but only if your skills are equal to the challenge. Galleries typically sell top-quality antique and reproduction furniture. If you have one close at hand, take a walk around inside. At first the content will intimidate you: Don't let it. If you can produce a high-quality piece of furniture, chances are you can also make a high-quality reproduction. Galleries are always looking for new talent, thus they represent a ready opportunity to make money.

Know Your Client

Before you get involved, research exactly what it is your prospect does. Study the

---

MISTAKE NUMBER 7: DON'T SHOW IT IF YOU CAN'T REPEAT IT

I've lost count of the number of times I've heard this: "Yeah, that's a nice piece, but is that what I can expect to receive if I give you an order? I've been screwed before." And most of them have. I know a couple of people personally who make a habit of showing one thing and delivering another. The samples they show are top-quality products made specifically to get the order. The pieces they deliver bear no resemblance to them, either in quality or appearance. It's people like this that give us all a bad name. Needless to say, they don't get many repeat orders.

pieces on display. Study the prices being asked. Talk to the sales staff. The more you know, the more prepared you'll be when you make your approach. Some galleries are small; some resemble shopping malls and have large numbers of dealers pushing everything from modern to Colonial furniture, and from textiles to fine art. Either way, the gallery is a unique opportunity to expand your business, your product range and your skills.

The Product

Gallery owners are always looking for something new. They have a tough time keeping the place stocked with attractive pieces, old or new. And, because prices are generally very high in this type of outlet, they rely on the range of products to attract customers. To begin with, I scoured books on antique furniture for ideas. I spent many long hours in the local library. The oval tavern table in my book *Building Classic Antique Furniture With Pine* (Popular Woodworking Books, 1997) was the result of that search—and was the first piece I ever sold to a gallery. It's a complicated piece to build, but attractive, and it opened the door to a new and lucrative outlet. Since that first sale, I've sold an assortment of reproductions to that gallery, all at a tidy profit.

Quality

Needless to say, the gallery will expect a first-class piece of work. Joints must be clean and tight, proportions must be just right, everything must be square and the finish must be exceptional. Reproduction furniture poses a challenge to begin with; to offer it for sale to an outlet of this caliber poses another. Your workmanship will be scrutinized, and the finish will be criticized. If you can pass the test, however, the extra profit, the unique feeling of satisfaction and pride, and the enjoyment you'll receive from building such a project will make it all worthwhile.

Pricing for the Gallery

The extra work, the time you'll spend on the finish, the type of buyer you'll be dealing with, the type of product itself and many more considerations demand you make each piece worthwhile. Prices in galleries generally reflect an upscale clientele. Your prices must increase accordingly. My advice is to add up to 25 percent to the price of a standard piece, and up to 50 percent for one that's custom built.

Are Galleries Worth the Hassle?

That, my friend, is a question only you can answer. I have found galleries to be a profitable outlet for me. I've found working with the owners to be fun, and I always enjoy building a new reproduction piece: It's what I do best. However, I wouldn't want to make a career of them. I've lost count of the number of pieces I've had to take back to the shop, not because of mistakes or poor workmanship,

but to make minute changes to the finish; it's always the finish. The gallery owner is often a knowledgeable antique dealer and thinks he knows his finishes. In reality, however, an authentic reproduction antique finish is a subjective thing that varies greatly from one dealer to another and from one craftsman to the next. Only time and an in-depth knowledge of your client's likes and dislikes will smooth the way. Even so, galleries do represent an important part of my business; so they could yours.

FINE FURNITURE STORES

These stores represent yet another profitable outlet for the independent furniture builder. By *fine furniture store* I don't mean the expensive chains, but rather the small, independently owned store you'll usually find in an older part of town. The furniture is often unique and expensive, targeted toward the affluent client (rather than you and me). As with the gallery, this type of owner will be looking for something different, probably a reproduction. Again, the quality will be more important than the price, which will often be higher than that asked for a similar piece in a gallery. These people are easy to approach, but generally more difficult to sell, and they are just as discerning as gallery owners. I've dealt with them on and off over the years, and they do, even today, represent a small part of my business. Your

buyer here will be looking for the unusual. It will be made from hardwood and superbly finished, and he will not usually consider anything the trade likes to call *primitive*: Shaker, Early American and so on. This buyer will be looking for reproduction Sheraton, Hepplewhite, Chippendale and the like: Fun to build, but often taking more time, and ultimately costing more than you can recover, even at the higher price the fine store owner is prepared to pay. I find I can only afford to supply small pieces to this type of outlet: Pembroke tables, sewing tables, coffee tables, small chests of drawers, etc. You will, however, gain something more from dealing with this type of business: prestige and reputation, both of which will take you a long way along the road to success. It never hurts to do a little name-dropping, and having the most exclusive store in town on your list of clients will do much for your reputation.

INTERIOR DESIGNERS

This type of buyer offers only a limited opportunity. You'll find them listed in the yellow pages. Almost all of the pieces you build will be custom designed and one of a kind. You'll need to be able to read a drawing, often not a professional one, and you'll need to be able to work closely with the designer: make changes to structure and finish, scrap the piece and start over, strip one finish and replace it with another and so on. In other words, if you can work well under constant supervision, this type of outlet might just be for you.

ARCHITECTS

Architects, like interior designers, can also represent a good source of business, but only intermittently. They don't generally buy furniture on a grand scale the way designers do, and what they do buy is almost always functional and modern. Again, however, it will often be custom designed and one of a kind. Get your money upfront. It's not unheard of for an architect to change his mind and reject a piece out of hand. Prices should reflect the extra work you'll be required to do.

chapter four

HOW TO DEVELOP YOUR OWN SALES AND MARKETING

Sales and marketing are two very different things: *Marketing* is what you do to get the word out; *sales* is what you do to move a product from your place to theirs. Simple? In concept, yes. In practice, no.

Here's something worth thinking about: Nothing happens until somebody sells something. That's a very deep and interesting statement. It means that the world turns on the art of the sale. It's timeless. Until someone sold something to someone else, there was nothing: no future, no past, no prospects and nothing to look forward to. The art of the sale is the solution to the problem and the cause of it. You are involved in buying and selling every day of your life, and I don't mean a trip to the grocery store. Sell someone an idea and you reap the benefits; sell someone on your skills and personality and you get the job. And so it goes. In fact, there's rarely a time when you open your mouth that you're not trying to sell someone on something. And, believe it or not, we are all very good at it; we just don't realize it. To be successful in business, all you have to do is take the concept one step further; raise it to the level of consciousness.

To do that, you'll need to acquire some basic tools and to understand some basic principles. Let's look at the principles first.

BUILDING PERSONAL RELATIONSHIPS

Personal relationships are the cornerstones of a successful business. At the risk of boring you, I'll repeat the fundamental maxim of sales and selling: People only buy from people they like. From day one, from the first moment you meet your prospective client, the building of your personal relationship should begin. You quickly must progress from Mr. This or Ms. That to a first-name relationship—on both sides. The moment your client begins to address you by your first name, you'll know your relationship has passed into stage two, and that a friendship is about to blossom.

KNOW YOUR COMPETITION

This applies to anyone selling a product, but in our case we have little true competition. By *true* I mean *direct* competition, other people in your own hometown making furniture for sale. Your competition probably will be the large furniture manufacturers or the local craft community. Even so, you'll need to learn all you can about the way things are done in the trade, how pricing is structured, how orders are placed and received, the quality of competing products, delivery practices and so on. The more you know, the better you'll be able to penetrate the marketplace.

BASIC SALES TECHNIQUES

The basic sale is made over a set series of steps: the presentation, the close, answering objections and writing the order. Each is important to achieving the desired goal.

THE PRESENTATION

Most sales presentations include a demonstration of some sort; yours will too. To make an effective sales presentation, you'll need some sales tools. These will include a sample of your work and a portfolio of photographs (more about that later).

Get In Touch With the Right Person

The first thing you should know about an effective sales presentation is that you shouldn't make it to the wrong person. There's nothing more frustrating than going through your stuff only to find out that the person in front of you is unable to buy. You can make the finest presentation ever, and it will be wasted if it's made to the wrong person. How can you tell if you're selling to the right person? Ask. "Can I speak to the person who does the buying?" or "Can I talk to the owner, please?"

Show the Product

You'll begin your presentation by explaining who you are and what you do. At the same time you begin your explanation,

open your portfolio and put it in front of your prospect: Don't ask him if he'd like to see it—show him. As you turn the pages, don't explain what he's seeing, because he already knows. Buyers get very annoyed when you explain the obvious. They think you think they're stupid.

Ask Questions

Do ask questions: Do you sell any of these? Is this sort of thing popular with your customers? And so on. These questions can lead to a sale.

He Will Ask Questions

This, too, is an important part of a sales presentation. If your potential buyer asks questions about any of the items he sees in your book, he's interested. A question from a prospect is a buying signal.

Buying Signals

These come in many forms, but mostly in the form of a question. The most obvious of these is: How much is it? Others can go like this: Can I get it in cherry? How is it finished? What's your minimum order? How many do I have to buy? What's your lead time? And so on. Buying signals should be answered with a closing question (more on that later).

Show the Sample

Finally, you'll come to a picture in your portfolio that will trigger the sample you have in your vehicle. When you reach that

page, tell your prospect you have one outside you'd like him to see.

CLOSING THE SALE

Selling is a game. In a selling situation, someone always wins and someone always loses: He buys and you win; you fail to close the sale and he wins. A sales presentation is rather like two combatants squaring off in combat. It's a cut-and-thrust situation with one opponent probing the weaknesses of the other—and it's fun. Becoming a great player is the way to success in making money making furniture.

Them That Don't Ask, Don't Get!

Closing the sale means asking for the order. There are a number of ways you can do it, but do it you must. If you only learn one thing from this chapter, it had better be this: If you don't ask your customer to buy, he won't. He might want it and the price might be right, but if you don't ask him to buy, you'll lose the sale. Not asking for the order is the single biggest mistake a salesman can make. Books have been written on this subject alone.

What Is a Closing Question?

A closing question is any question the answer to which indicates the customer has bought. For example, a customer might ask you, "Can I get it in green?" Your first reaction when asked a question like this will be to say *yes*. If you do, the chances

are you'll lose the sale. Answer his question with a closing question of your own, like this: Do you want it in green? If he says *yes*, he's bought it: Write the order. The answer to your question was *yes*, an indication that your customer has bought. You closed the sale.

Shut Up and Wait

This also is one of the most important principles of salesmanship. Whenever you ask a closing question, shut up, look your prospect in the eye—and wait for him to answer. The first one to speak loses! This is the oldest game in the business. The wait can seem interminable, but don't under any circumstances be the first to crack. If you speak first you let him off the hook, and the sale will be lost.

Two Questions You Can Count On

There are literally thousands of closing questions, and I'm not going into them all here. There are just a couple that will work for you 90 percent of the time. They are simple: "Can I make one for you to try?" or "It will take me a couple of weeks to make one of those. Will that be OK?" A *yes* to either question and you've made the sale. But don't stop there. Write the order and move on to the next item. Once the ice is broken and the customer has started to buy, more sales will come easily.

You Can Also Count On This

A closing question will almost always—no, will *always*—bring only one response: How much is it? You'd better know the answer. At this point in the relationship between buyer and seller, price is one of the most important considerations. Answer the question confidently: Never show apology in your tone of voice. If you don't believe your piece is worth its price, it's probably not, and you'll let your prospect know it by how you answer the question.

Now, your price probably will be too high, whatever it is. At least, that's what your prospect will tell you. And that's OK, as long as you know your limits. It's OK to lower your price a little—it's expected—but don't give your work away. If you feel your price is right, don't be afraid to stand fast. Your prospect may not buy that particular piece, but he will respect you for your stand.

Price Should Be Flexible

Having said you should stand your ground on price, there will be times when you can lower your price to meet an unusual situation. But this should not be done until you've established a pattern of price integrity.

OBJECTIONS

Unless you know better, objections can be the most daunting part of the sales process. Objections come in a variety of ways. They are not, however, always all they seem. Unless the buyer tells you flat out that he's not going to buy, objections are buying signals.

Price

If there's any objection, it will usually be that your price is too high. And to most people that objection will signal the end of the presentation—and a lost sale. It shouldn't. When a prospect tells you your price is too high, he isn't telling you he won't buy. What he's really saying is this: That's more than I wanted to pay, but if you can come down a bit, or tell me why it's worth that much money, I might buy.

Don't Give In

Don't lower your price unless that was part of your original plan. If you do, you set yourself up for the future. Once you lower your price, you'll be expected to do so forevermore.

Explain Value for Money

Tell the buyer why your price is what it is, and then ask for the order again. If a piece is made from solid wood, it's worth more than one made from MDF. If it's made of cherry instead of pine, it worth more money. If the design is unique, it's worth more money. If you've been asked to rush deliver, it's worth more money. And so on.

I Buy Only From Large Manufacturers

This one you'll hear a lot. Ask him why. This is part of knowing the competition.

Unless you know what he's thinking, you can't persuade him to buy from you. Remember, he hasn't said he won't buy from you. What he's really said is: Tell me why I should buy from you, and I will.

Personal Service

This is, of course, the main reason he should buy from you. You're local. He can get in touch with you whenever he likes. He will be dealing with a warm body rather than a disembodied voice on the telephone. You can fix problems as they arise. You can supply one-off orders, custom-built pieces and so on. There are a great many reasons why it is advantageous for a buyer to deal directly with you.

I've Been Screwed Before

I mentioned this objection briefly in the sidebar on page 34. It has to do with delivering exactly what you've promised or shown. When you first hear this one you might think you've hit a brick wall and that a sale is impossible. Not so. Actually, it's a fairly easy objection to overcome. Say something like: "I understand how you feel. How about this? Pick out a piece you like and I'll make it for you—no obligations. If it's not up to your standards, you don't have to pay for it. I'll take it away. That way you have nothing to lose. How about it?" Now shut up and wait for the answer. Put it like this, and you'll rarely leave without an order.

No Objections, No Sale

There are many more objections you'll hear over the years. They shouldn't be taken as a deterrent. It's better for you to get objections than it is to deal with someone who won't talk at all. Answer the objection, and then close again.

DON'T LEAVE WITHOUT AN ORDER

This, of course, is not always possible. Many times it will take more than one visit to secure an order. One fine furniture store I deal with had me return *five times* before the buyer gave me a small trial order. It's part of the game. And some buyers simply like to know that you'll be around for a while if they decide to buy from you. Whatever the reason, you should always try to leave with an order for something, even if just a small piece. Once the door is open, it's easy to proceed on through.

DON'T SHOW WHAT YOU CAN'T PRODUCE

This simply means that you shouldn't offer to build a piece that's beyond your skills. Obvious? Yes, but you'd be surprised how easy to is say *yes* when you know you should be saying *no*. The bad part about falling into the *yes* trap is you're sure to lose credibility with your client, and you will spend many restless hours worrying about something you can't produce, at least in an acceptable form.

DON'T TAKE ON TOO MUCH

It's easy to get carried away and take on more than you can handle. It's difficult to say *no* when a buyer is on a roll. The problem is you're only a one-man shop and, even with the best of intentions, if you take on too much, deliveries will not be on time, and your customer will be upset. It's better to walk away with a small order, turn it in on time and continue your relationship with another small order. This way you'll keep your clients.

A THICK SKIN

In sales you'll need a thick skin. This means you must be able to handle rejection. At first, most of your interviews will not produce orders. You'll hear the word *no* many times over, and you'll need to be able to accept it without taking it personally. Almost always, at least in the early days, it comes because your prospect doesn't know you—because there's no personal relationship. People only buy from people they like. Remember?

HANG IN THERE

As I've mentioned before, many of your sales will be made only after you've called on a prospective client a number of times. It's part of the game. Hang in there and try to put the relationship on a first-name basis, and sooner or later you will get an order. What you do with it will determine the quality of your relationship with that particular client forevermore.

SALES TOOLS

In the early days your sales kit will consist of three parts, all marketing tools: business cards and some simple flyers, a couple of samples of your work and a portfolio of photographs. In the beginning, your portfolio will probably contain only one or two photographs, but that doesn't matter. It will grow right along with your business.

Business Cards

These little jewels are an essential part of your sales kit. They can do a lot for you, and you can do a lot with them. A bifold card can work like a minibrochure. Your name, address and phone number go on the front, and a sales blurb can go on the inside. Some people simply list the products they make on the inside; others explain that they build custom furniture and include a short list. Buy your cards by the thousand and hand them out everywhere. Every chance meeting is an opportunity to get the word out. Visit the bank, give the teller a card. Visit the drugstore, give the salesperson a card. If you get only one hit from every hundred cards, a thousand will bring in ten new customers, and if each new customer talks to five or six friends, the word will quickly spread.

Your Portfolio

Your samples will lead to orders. Photograph everything you make. Even before you begin to make furniture for sale, you

should take photographs of everything you make. If you can, have your pieces photographed professionally. Each piece should be presented as favorably as possible. If you can't afford to have the photographs made by a pro, do it yourself, outside in the open, under an overcast sky. An overcast day will produce no shadows, and thus your pictures will be less contrasty. Move in close and fill the picture. There's nothing worse than a photograph of a tiny piece way off in the distance. Your work will be difficult to see, and the picture will do you little or no service.

Presentation Is Everything

Just as you must do a professional job of building and finishing a piece of furniture, you must do a professional job of presenting your pictures. Invest in a good-quality photo album. If you can, have your photographs enlarged to $8'' \times 10''$. Place only one or two pictures on each page.

Keep Your Prices to Yourself

Your price list should be kept in a place other than your portfolio. I found this out very early in my career. I had a typed list right in the front of my book. Guess where my prospect wanted to start looking. Yes, right there with the prices. You can't give prices before you show the work. They will always be too high, and the interview may well end right there.

Finally

Always maintain a positive attitude. Be enthusiastic about your work and about the pieces in your portfolio.

The First Sale Is Always to Yourself
Here's a little maxim you will do well to remember. First, take the word *enthusiasm*, then look at the last four letters: *IASM*. These are letters you should live by. They stand for *I Am Sold Myself*.

WORK SAMPLES

In my fledgling period I used a blanket chest as my sample: It was 36″ long, 18″ high and 18″ wide, just like the one in the project section. I figured such a piece would be popular with most types of dealers and outlets, and I was right. Now this wasn't your average, run-of-the-mill blanket chest. It was a finely built piece, constructed using dovetail joints and reproduction hardware. It was made of furniture-grade pine, lightly stained and superbly finished; you couldn't buy anything quite like it anywhere. It was built to get attention. I could have sold that piece many times over, but I didn't. In the end I lost count of the number of times I showed it. That chest shepherded me into the business. It gave prospective buyers an idea of my skills. Most of my orders were, however, for items other than a blanket chest, and that enabled me to build the other part of my sales kit: the portfolio of photographs. By the way, the chests I delivered were always of a quality equal to that of the sample.

Stick Out Your Chest
I'm not saying you should use a chest as I did. You will, however, need to come up with something. I found the chest easy to transport and easy to show, and it incorporated many of the fine construction features furniture dealers like to see. Maybe it will work for you too.

TOOLS AND EQUIPMENT YOU'LL NEED

If you want to make money making furniture, you'll need to be able to work as efficiently as possible. And that means you'll need to tool up. True, you can make money with only the most rudimentary tools, even with just a few hand tools if you like, but you won't make much money, and you certainly won't be able to make a living. Yes, I know, Messrs. Sheraton, Hepplewhite and Chippendale did quite nicely. But times are different now. The pressures and demands of the modern environment will not allow the three months required to build a furniture masterpiece. And no matter what the purists may say, I'm sure the big three would have had shops full of power tools that would have made even Norm Abram envious, had they been available.

Please bear in mind that the tools and accessories listed below are only suggestions for what I consider to be essential to a well-rounded one-man shop. You could certainly do quite well with less. Where I've listed specific manufacturers, I've done so because I'm completely familiar with their products. Again, however, these are only suggestions. Use whatever works best for you.

THE BASICS

To begin with, you can get by with just the basics, a table saw and a couple of routers.

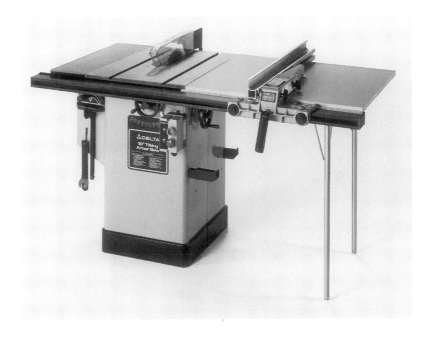

That's about how I began. It won't be long, however, before the restrictions imposed by the lack of a full range of power tools begin to make themselves evident. Time will be lost changing bits and blades, trying to do half a dozen jobs on one machine that could be done so much easier with just a couple more. When I began making furniture for money, my shop consisted of the following: a new Craftsman 10″ contractor's saw, a small 10″ table saw, two Sears cordless drill motors, two Sears routers and a half-dozen router bits. Believe it or not, it was getting the job done—but barely. I was struggling.

TABLE SAW
This *Delta* contractor's saw is plenty to get you started. As you progress in your work, you may find you need to upgrade to a more powerful cabinet-type saw.

JOINTER

A jointer with a 6″ bed provides you with a lot of versatility and a variety of jointing options. This type of jointer is more powerful and safer than smaller models.

PLANER

This powerful *Delta* planer will meet all your planing needs.

At that point I sat down and analyzed my situation. What was I trying to do? And how serious was I? When I had answered those questions, I analyzed the market and decided that an assortment of Delta

and Porter Cable stationary and portable power tools would fulfill all my needs. Next, I drew up a list of what I thought I might need to do the job as efficiently as possible. Then, having made the list, I bit the bullet and acquired what I thought would be the dream workshop.

A MULTIFACETED DREAM SHOP

The following sections list what I feel are the minimum requirements for an efficient one-man furniture shop. Some of the tools you may already own, and that's fine. Some you may feel to be an unnecessary luxury, and that's fine too. And you may not be able to afford to buy the items you need more than one at a time—also fine. My best advice is to do what you can as soon as you can, and continue to tool up as your earnings increase. I've listed the tools and explained the reasons for their inclusion by order of merit: Those I consider to be indispensable first, followed in order by those to be acquired at a later date.

Stationary Power Tools

Delta Cabinet or Contractor's 10″ Table Saw. I decided on Delta simply because of their advanced rip-fence system. The fence can be reversed, switched and turned into a guide stop with just the twist of a couple of knobs. Also, the miter gauge is keyed to its slot, making it much easier to crosscut wide boards. Cost: $850 and up.

SHAPER

A shaper makes raised-panel doors and custom moldings a snap. It is a versatile and safe machine that will do a lot more than your router table.

Delta 6″ Deluxe Jointer (an 8″ version would be even better). It wasn't until I acquired one of these marvelous and versatile tools that I realized how indispensable it is. If you already have one, you know what I mean. If you don't, you're in for a treat. If only to make great joints between boards, this tool ranks alongside the table saw as a must have. Cost: $450 and up.

Planer (12″ or larger). If you're serious about making money making furniture, you will find this item to be indispensable. Within a couple of months it will have earned back its cost in savings on board stock alone. You can buy furniture-grade pine and other unfinished stock for far less than you can in finished

form. Not only that, your range will expand; thin boards will become a reality, not just a dream. Cost: $350 and up.

Dedicated Mortising Machine. This probably would not be on most people's list as an essential member of the workshop team, but it should be. Some people say an attachment for a drill press will do just as well. Not true. The attachments just don't work the way they are supposed to, and are difficult to set up and take down. Why do you need a mortising

BAND SAW

A small, benchtop band saw will only frustrate the woodworker who will be using it to make money. Invest in a two-wheel type like this one with a large throat capacity.

DUST COLLECTOR
This is an essential tool in any workshop.

DRILL PRESS ▶
This tool is excellent for cutting your own screw plugs, angled drilling and some sanding operations. You can buy a mortising attachment that turns your drill press into a mortising machine.

machine? As you make more and more furniture, you'll naturally make more and more mortises; the mortise-and-tenon joint is by far the best way to build tables, chairs and the like. The dedicated machine makes the operation a quick and easyprocess without a lot of hassle.

Shaper. I don't have one, preferring a home-built router table instead, but if you can afford one, there's no doubt it would be a great asset to your endeavors. Cost: $280 and up.

Band Saw (the bigger, the better). I suggest nothing less than a 14″ model, perhaps with a 6″ height extension. This

is one of the most indispensable tools in the shop. I do a great deal of work on my Delta machine, even resawing; you've got to have one. Cost: $650 and up.

Dust Collector. This one is a must, especially as you're going to be spending long hours in the shop. Wood dust can

be irritating at best, and downright dangerous at worst: Get rid of it. Cost: $200 and up.

Drill Press. If you don't have one, you should. You can't drill an accurate hole with a handheld machine. Cost: $250 and up.

Lathe. You just can't imagine how much you'll appreciate this machine once you've learned how to use it. First, it will greatly increase your range. You'll be able to make nicely turned, elegant legs for your tables. Second, it's great fun just to spend an hour or two quietly playing, turning bits of scrap stock into pretty, but mostly useless, bits and pieces of objets d'art. You wouldn't believe the number of rolling pins my wife owns. (Hey, we all need to relax sometimes.) Cost: $450 and up.

Radial Arm Saw. Although not an essential, you will really appreciate the extra scope and efficiency this versatile tool will bring to your shop. It's much more than an elaborate cutoff saw. You can dado, miter, compound miter, rip and even route with a radial arm. I left this one off my initial list of goodies, but I have a Delta machine now and wouldn't part with it. Cost: You can buy a small, 8″ radial arm saw at Sears, and you can buy a more powerful 10″ saw there too. They cost about $350 and $550, respectively. How good they are I couldn't say. A Delta machine will cost $650 and up.

Spindle Sander. For years I went

RADIAL ARM SAW
This versatile machine can do a lot more than simply cut off boards.

without one of these, thinking them to be an expensive luxury. I have one now, and it's become indispensable. It makes short work of sanding compound curves, and

SPINDLE SANDER
A great addition to your sanding department, and much better than the drums you attach to a drill press.

COMPOUND MITER SAW

These saws have changed the way woodworkers think about cutting moldings and angles. A very handy saw to have if you don't already have a radial arm saw.

LATHE

This is a dedicated *Delta* lathe with all the bells and whistles. You'll need to develop your lathe skills eventually.

turns a rough-looking shape into a thing of beauty. Cost: $300 and up.

Compound Miter Saw. Yes, you can cut most of your miters on the table saw, and you can even cut compound miters on a radial arm saw, but nothing can quite compare with a machine designed and dedicated to this one specific job; it makes a terrific chop saw too. Cost: $250 and up.

Sanding Center. I did without one of these for a long time too. I made do with a belt sander turned upside down, which was not the best of solutions. Today, I own a Delta 6″ × 48″ sanding center with a 12″ disk. However did I do without it? Cost:

Small units can be purchased for as little $200; bigger units can run $800 and up.

These stationary tools are those I consider to be the essentials of an efficient one-man shop. With these I can perform almost any woodworking technique you can imagine, and I can do it quickly and with confidence. I can turn out nice, high-quality pieces in a minimum of time.

Portable Power Tools

Oh boy. If you're a gadget freak like me, you shouldn't be reading this. There's not a portable power tool I wouldn't like to have, if only to play with. The truth is,

SANDING CENTER

You can use the disc sander to straighten edges before butt-jointing boards.

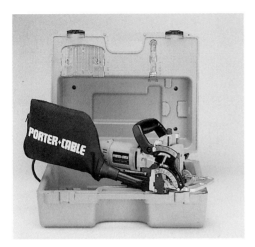

BISCUIT JOINTER
These are much easier than dowels to use when gluing up large panels for tabletops and are incomparable for angled or butt-joint edge joining.

2.5 (AND MORE) HP ROUTER
If you are using your router a lot, you'll need a powerful model that will last.

1.5 HP ROUTER
This tool is all the router you'll need for weekend woodworking.

however, that the best brands are expensive, and few of us can afford to indulge in wild buying just for the pleasure of it. These, then, are the tools I consider to be essential to an efficient shop. With one or two exceptions, I use Porter Cable tools exclusively. Although they can be on the

expensive side, I find the quality, reliability and long life make them well worth the extra cost. Again, they are listed in order of importance.

Biscuit Jointer. How did we ever get along without this wonderful, inexpensive little tool? For years I did without. Then I bought a crazy little attachment for my old Sears router and things improved, just a bit. I acquired my Porter Cable machine several years ago, and it moved me into a new dimension of woodworking. Until recently, I even used it when making raised-panel doors, for joining the rails and styles. You've got to have one. Cost: $150 and up.

Routers (1.5 horsepower). You can't have enough of these. At the very least you need two: a standard fixed model and one with a plunge base interchangeable with a fixed base. Cost: You can buy inexpensive Sears models for around $65; a 1.5 hp Porter Cable unit will run $185 and up.

BELT SANDER

Even if you have a sanding center, you'll need a portable belt sander for flattening tabletops and removing glue from panels.

Routers (2.5 horsepower and up). You'll need at least one of these—two is ideal—to enable you to use the larger bits and to put into your router table (again for use with the larger bits). Cost: $220 and up.

Belt Sander. This is another essential tool. Don't buy an inexpensive brand. It won't last ten minutes, and you'll have to work physically hard to remove any amount of material. I consider a $3'' \times 24''$ Porter Cable or a similar machine to be the very minimum to get the job done quickly, efficiently and with as little physical exertion as possible. The Porter Cable model is heavy enough to do the work without the application of pressure by its operator. Cost: You can expect to pay $220 and up for one, but it will be worth its weight in gold. A lightweight Sears $3'' \times 21''$ sander will cost $55 and up, and it will make a man of you.

Random Orbital Sander. Again, don't buy a cheap model; the finish will leave a lot to be desired, and personally I hate hand sanding. Porter Cable, DeWalt and several other premium units all do excellent work and will save you time and

RANDOM-ORBIT SANDER

These are a much improved design over the old fixed-orbit sanders that left swirls in your work.

CORDLESS DRILLS

How did we ever get along without these? Indispensable for any shop.

money in the long run. Cost: $90 and up.

Cordless Drill Motor. Get two if you can, of at least 9.5 volts. The attributes of a good cordless drill are self-evident and do not need explaining here. Cost: $120 and up for a good one.

Detail Sander. Do you need one of these little jewels? No, of course not, but they sure are nice. I use mine all the time. Cost: $85 and up.

Nonpower Tools and Jigs

Router Table. I started out, as many of you will, with a small Craftsman table and the machine that went with it. I soon

found, however, that it severely limited my scope: For instance, I couldn't use bits with ½″ shanks, and I certainly couldn't use anything larger than a ½″ roundover bit. The answer, then, was to build my own. The one I use now can take bits up to 3″ in diameter. I can raise panels, profile, machine rails and stiles and much more. There are any number of plans on the market, so I won't bore you with how I made mine. Suffice it say, you should build something that will cover all your needs.

Router Bits. I'm not going to go into great detail here, but you do need a com-

ROUTER TABLE
You can either build your own or buy a commercial model.

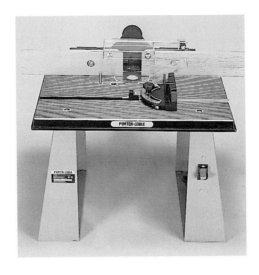

BIT SET
This bit set is *Jesada's Roundover Kit* with bits from ¼″ to 1″. The set on the right is their master kit—all you need to make money making furniture.

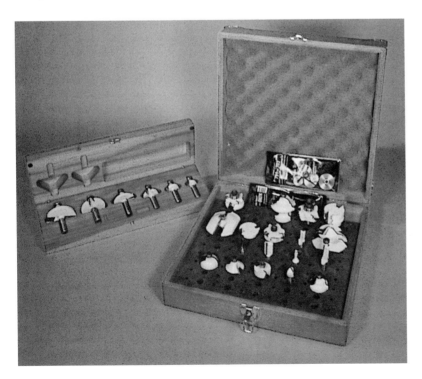

prehensive assortment, especially if you're going to do specialized work such as raised-panel doors and the like. To cover your needs, I suggest you purchase a couple of assortments from Jesada Tools in Florida: The Router Bit Magic Set for

$699 includes all you need for rabbeting, flush trimming, mortising, rounding, v-grooving, chamfering, fancy edging, lock jointing, lock mitering, profiling, panel raising, rails and stiles and even inlaying: It's a comprehensive, all-round assortment. To complete your bit lineup, consider another Jesada assortment: the Six Bit Roundover Set for $199. The set includes six roundover bits, ¼″ through 1″, and a bearing set that converts them to beading bits (12 for the price of 6). I use these bits on a day-to-day basis and find them to be first-quality tools: They stay sharp and cut smoothly. What more can you ask.

Clamps. Get rid of all those wimpy little bar clamps and buy yourself some Bessey K-Body clamps. Start out with four 24″, four 36″, four 48″ and a couple more, as long as you can afford them, and then build on that. If you're going to build high-quality furniture for sale, you need good clamps, especially if you're going to be building panels and the like. I'll say no more than this: Good clamps are the secret to success in woodworking.

Dovetail Jig. Forget the little 12″ models you can buy at the hardware store; they just won't do a proper job. I'm lucky enough to own a Leigh system, and it is one of the best acquisitions I have in my shop. It has a 24″ range that means I can build beautiful chests, drawers and cabinets I couldn't make with one of those little plastic devices you see advertised for $50 and up. Yes, I've used one of those. I

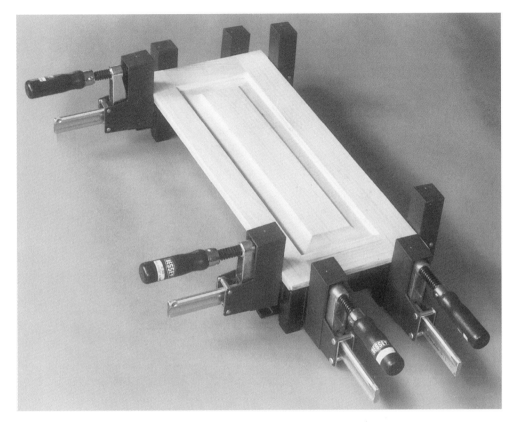

CLAMPS
You can never own enough good quality clamps.

found it difficult to work with, and the joints left a lot to be desired. The Leigh system will set you back $600 or more—bits included—but it's an investment that will pay you back a thousandfold. The appearance of your joints alone will often clinch the sale for you.

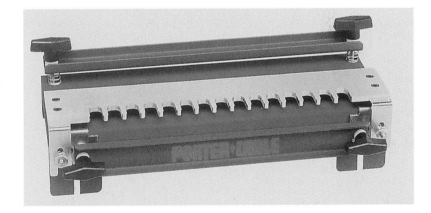

DOVETAIL JIG
This solid *Porter Cable* jig will outlast you.

FINDING YOUR MATERIALS

You will, of course, be expected to produce furniture using all sorts of hardwood. But for simplicity, we'll keep the variety to a minimum. One thing before we get into specifics: Never buy lumber in bulk. Buy only what you think you'll need to complete the next four or five projects. There's simply no point in keeping money tied up in large quantities of lumber, even if it is cheaper to buy it that way.

PINE

This is the quintessential material for those beginning a career making money making furniture. It's easy to get hold of, relatively inexpensive, easy to work and forgiving. It's also easy to finish and presents an attractive appearance.

Variety

Pine comes in a variety of forms. There's Eastern white pine, Southern white and yellow pine, parana pine, spruce and fir. The easiest to come by are the Eastern and Southern varieties. You can find these in various forms in your local hardware store for around a dollar or so per board foot. Not so easily come by is parana pine. Most of it comes from South America and is quite expensive. It is,

however, one of the best mediums for making attractive furniture. Spruce can usually be found in your local builder's supply. It's a very clean stock with few knots. It is, however, much softer than the other members of the pine family, the surface tends to fur up when sanded and it's also quite expensive. Some of the firs are nice to work with. They present a nice clean look, but once again, they are fairly expensive, and using them will cut deep into your profit margin.

Local Stock

For the beginner, the local hardware store may be the best place to begin. True, it won't be the cheapest, but with a little persuasion, you may be able to talk the manager into giving you a discount. You should be aware, however, that the pine you'll buy in this type of outlet will inevitably be what's known as *shelving board*. It comes in various grades and lengths of $1'' \times 12''$ board that actually turns out to be $\frac{3}{4}'' \times 11\frac{1}{4}''$. You'll need to be picky when making your purchases. Look for nice clean boards free from splits and breaks. It should also have been stored inside the building, not outside on the dock where it will have absorbed all the moisture in the atmosphere. Sometimes you can find this sort of stock in a local builder's supply. They may, however, not want to deal with you as a member of the public. If you can persuade them to deal, you'll probably be able to buy your stock at a slightly better price.

Furniture-Grade Pine

This is the best type of stock for making furniture. I use it in large quantities. You'll find it only at a lumberyard/sawmill. It's kiln dried to 10 percent moisture or less, warpfree and easy to work. It does, however, almost always come rough-sawn, so you'll need to own a planer of some sort. Yes, you can have it finished at the yard, but they'll charge from 10 to 15 cents per board foot for doing it.

Better is Often Cheaper

Believe it or not, furniture-grade pine can cost quite a lot less than the shelving board I mentioned. I've yet to find a grade-two shelving board for less than $1.20 per board foot—grade three is the what you'll usually find at about $1.00 per foot—but I can buy furniture grade for less than 70 cents. Most often it will come in various lengths from 6' to 14', in various widths from 4" to 15", and in thicknesses exceeding 1⅛", which means there's quite a bit of work to do before it can be turned into usable stock, but which also means you'll have a ready supply of thicker stock: ¾" up to 1", finished. And that's great for making tabletops, desktops and more.

Legs and Such

The lumberyard is also the only place where you'll be able to purchase decent stock from which to make legs. True, you can use 2×4s or 4×4s bought at the local hardware store, but it's usually of a different variety, and when two pieces of thinner stock are glued together to make a chunk large enough to use, you can see the joint, which is not pretty.

Again, furniture-grade or rough stock bought at the lumberyard is the answer. You can buy thick stock from 4/4 all the way up to 12/4 and even larger. If it's kiln dried, you've got the best of all worlds. The stock will be clean, will be unlikely to split and will work beautifully. Best of all, your leg material will match that used for the rest of the construction.

OAK

This is the second medium of choice for making money making furniture. You'll make almost as much furniture from oak as you will from pine. It's popular with the public and sells well both as retail and to the trade. It's a tough, good-looking wood, but sometimes difficult to work. Two varieties are generally available: red oak and white oak.

Red Oak

This is the least expensive to buy and the easiest to find. Don't buy it from the local store unless you're prepared to pay through the nose. At some stores you can

expect to pay $5 and up per board foot for a clean piece of red oak; you can buy it at the lumberyard for a fifth of that.

At the lumberyard you'll be presented with a number of choices. The best-quality red oak is classed FAS: first and seconds. This means the board is pretty well clean and can be used almost as is—with a little finishing, of course. You can expect to pay $2.50 and up per board foot for FAS red oak: Don't do it. I use #1 common stock almost exclusively. Aside from a knot or two, and maybe the odd split, it's essentially the same as FAS. With a little planning and some judicious cutting, you can use every little piece. Best of all, you can buy #1 common red oak for as little as $1.10 per board foot, especially once you've established a relationship with the yard.

White Oak

This seems to be a superior form of oak, very similar to English oak that was used in Colonial times. The grain is straighter and finer, and lends itself more easily to carving than does its red brother. Unfortunately, it's not as easy to get hold of. You may be lucky and find some at your local lumberyard; if not, they will order some in for you. It will be expensive, and you really can't mix red and white.

SASSAFRAS

This is one of the oak look-alikes. It's a fairly soft wood with a greenish tinge, but it sands beautifully, stains well and is useful for working interiors: shelves and the like. I use quite a lot of it, especially for inexpensive cabinets, cupboards and bookshelves. You can find it at many lumberyards. FAS grade will cost almost as much as oak, but the lesser grades can cost quite a bit less. I use #3 common and pay only 40 cents a board foot for it. Again, judicious cutting reduces my scrap to almost nothing. One problem with this wood, however, is that the dust is an irritant: Be sure to wear a mask when milling it.

MAPLE

I don't use a lot of maple, simply because it's so expensive. When I do get a call for it, however, I usually buy soft maple at the lumberyard. I buy it unfinished—it's much cheaper—and plane it to thickness myself. The cost? Anywhere from $3.50 and up per board foot.

THE OTHER HARDWOODS

These I try to stay away from. Occasionally I will work with cherry and walnut, but the cost, even at the lumberyard, is prohibitive. Make a mistake when working with a nice piece of cherry and, for me at least, the despair I feel because I've ruined such a lovely piece of wood outweighs even the monetary loss. Try to avoid the expensive hardwoods if you can.

BE ON THE LOOKOUT

In chapter three (page 27) I mentioned the little weekly advertiser (newspaper) we have in our area. On a number of occasions I've found bargain parcels of lumber in this little jewel. One such was 850 board feet of poplar I picked up for $125. It was rough-sawn, but it had been stored in a basement for more than a year and thus was relatively dry. I turned that $125 into more than $5,000 worth of furniture.

Since then I've picked up small parcels of walnut, cherry and maple, all for around a dollar or so per board foot. It's out there if you're on the lookout.

PLYWOOD

You can save money on hardwood by using a faced plywood, but only where it won't show: sides of cabinets, shelves and the like. You can buy ¾″ oak-faced plywood at quite a savings over the real thing. You can also use maple-, cherry- and walnut-faced plywood, although it will be hard to find, and you'll probably have to get your lumberyard to special order it for you.

Bottoms and Backs

For these I use only the most inexpensive lauan plywood, ¼″ thick. It's still expensive for what it is, but it's all that's available. I pay anywhere from $10 per sheet at the lumberyard to $14 per sheet at the local hardware store.

WHAT'S GOOD FOR THE ENVIRONMENT . . .

I am, of course, talking about recycling. No, I'm not joining the ranks of the concerned: I'm talking about recycled lumber. Unfortunately, since the advent of Norm Abram and the New Yankee Workshop, recycled lumber is not as cheap as it once was. Still, you can find it almost everywhere, if you just go out of your way a little. Keep an eye out for new demolition sites, old buildings being remodeled and the like. Don't be afraid to drop in and talk to the powers that be. I've picked up some lovely old wood for no more than the cost of hauling it away. Unfortunately, those opportunities don't come along quite as frequently as they once did, but a faint heart never did win a fair lady: Take every opportunity you can. You may have to pay a little more than you'd like for your antique oak and pine, but the quality of the lumber will more than justify the extra cost and effort. They didn't use rubbish back in the good old days.

HARDWARE

I always use good-quality hardware, and so should you. The few pennies you'll save buying a cheap product are not worth the problems that always result from poor quality: Doors that don't close properly, pulls that fall apart in your fingers, screws that are so soft you can't drive them, and so and so on. You can save a little on good-quality hardware by buying in bulk; I don't. I prefer instead to go to one of the hardware giants and buy what I need as I need it. That way I don't tie up money in dead stock.

STAINS AND PAINTS

These I buy at my local paint supplier, and I always buy the best-quality products. For stain I use Minwax; for paint I use a proprietary brand that's made locally. By using the same supplier, I get a 20 percent discount over retail. I could probably do a little better by buying in bulk and direct, but again I buy only what I need when I need it, thus keeping money in my pocket and not on the shelf.

POLYURETHANES

Again, I use only a top-quality brand. What I lose up front on the cost of the product, I more than gain back in time saved and a high-quality finish. I also use the new two-in-one stain and polyurethane for some pieces. I buy these items at my local paint store in gallon quantities, at a discount of 20 percent.

VARNISHES AND SHELLACS

These are products I have to buy through the mail from one of the large mail-order houses: Woodworker's Supply is my primary source. I use three types: seedlac, buttonlac for an old-world look, and orange shellac for more conventional finishes. Again, I buy only what I need to keep me going for a month or so.

FASTENERS

For interior work—inside a cabinet—I use drywall screws. I buy them by the pound at the local hardware store—just five pounds at a time—in two lengths: $1\frac{1}{4}''$ and $1\frac{3}{4}''$. I never let one of these modern screws show, even where it would be permissible to do so: They just don't look right. I also use cut-steel nails on occasion. These are not as easily come by, but most builder's yards do carry them. And, of course, I do use a variety of finishing nails.

Other fasteners I use on a day-to-day basis are biscuits. These I buy through the mail by the thousand from companies like Trend Lines. I pay $19.99 for 1000 #20 biscuits. The prices charged by the local stores are prohibitive: as much as $4 for 50. By the way, I do not use the smaller sizes, preferring instead to cut down a #20: This gives me a bigger tenon and a larger gluing area.

SHOP CAREFULLY

No matter where you buy your materials, shop around for the best prices. Look in the yellow pages for the nearest lumberyards—and by lumberyards I mean commercial sawmills—and get quotes for everything you think you might need. The more you save, the more you'll earn. In the early days the savings will perhaps only be a dollar a two per unit, but those dollars tend to mount up over the course of a year. Try this: Say you get a quote for pine board of 99 cents a board foot at the local yard, and another of 89 cents at the lumberyard, a difference of 10 cents, and you buy 250 board feet at the lumberyard for a savings of $25. Make a note of the date, put the $25 in a can—a big can—and forget it. Do this on every product you buy. In some cases it may only be 50 cents you save. No matter. Fifty cents here, ten dollars there, a dollar on finishing nails, two dollars more on screws and so on: Drop it all in the can. Don't try to keep track of the savings. Do this for your first year and then open the can. I guarantee you'll get the surprise of your life. You'll find enough money in that can to take the whole family away for a weeklong vacation at a nice hotel. Try it.

chapter seven

FINANCING YOUR BUSINESS

If you can, try to get started without taking out a loan. The work will be difficult enough without taking on the extra burden. This means, of course, that you shouldn't quit your real job until you have enough money put away to get you through the first three months—even if you don't get a single order during that period.

BUILD A CUSHION

Of course, you will get orders, but that's not what I'm talking about. I'm talking about cushions, about the ability to survive, to go to work on a daily basis without the worry of where your next meal, the next board of lumber, the next pot of glue and so on is coming from. Just knowing you have the ability to keep the bills paid and food on the table for three months will provide peace of mind, which in itself is essential to making a success of a fledgling business.

DON'T QUIT YOUR REAL JOB

If your idea is simply to make extra money, you won't even be considering this step. If, however, your plan is to make a living, there's no reason why you can't build the basis of a successful small business in your spare time. True, you'll spend more hours working than you'd like, but if you enjoy woodworking, so what? The advantages of building a solid base before taking the giant step far outweigh the uncertainty that always accompanies a premature decision to plunge in at the deep end.

GETTING STARTED

When you do finally quit your job and head out into the business world on your own, all of the initial outlay should have been made: You should have stock—a reasonable supply of lumber—in hand enough to build perhaps a half-dozen large pieces; you should have purchased the basic supplies, tools and machines to produce a professional piece of furniture; your three-month cushion should be safely in the bank; and you should have a book of orders to carry you through the first six weeks.

SIX IN HAND

If you can take the plunge with a three-month cushion in the bank and a book of orders to take you through the first six weeks, financing your operation should not be a problem. The money should stay in the bank, to be touched only when absolutely needed—and it will be—and the profit you'll make on your orders should more than pay your way. A loan should not be a part of the plan, at least not at this stage.

IF YOU NEED A LITTLE HELP

Don't be afraid to open accounts with your suppliers. These alone will allow you to operate for 30 to 45 days on other people's money. Be sure to pay your bills on time, though. Lose your good credit rating, and you'll find life in the commercial future tough indeed.

OPM—OTHER PEOPLE'S MONEY

And talking of other people's money, if you truly find you can't make it without some outside financing, you still can make it without taking on a long-term loan. The answer just might already lie in your wallet. Yes, I'm talking about credit cards.

Credit Cards

Credit cards can make life in business a whole lot more tolerable. They can, if the need arises, even put food on the table. Most grocery stores take them these days, but that wasn't exactly what I had in mind. I was thinking of financing the day-to-day workings of your one-man business— don't even consider paying an employee using credit cards. There are a couple of ways you can do this. The most obvious way is to charge tools and materials as you

need them. The other way is a little farther reaching, and will provide limited liquidity: You can get a cash advance on your cards. So, how far can you go using plastic?

Suppose you have a couple of Visa/MasterCards and an American Express card. The American Express probably will provide high-end, short-term credit. You can buy expensive machines, etc., without the inconvenience of going to the bank for the money. You should be aware, however, that this is a *very* short-term option. You will have, at best, five weeks to pay your bill before the letters start arriving. And you can believe me when I tell you that American Express will cut you off in a heartbeat if you're late making your payments. If that happens, your good credit rating will, as they say, be gone with the wind.

Beyond the immediacy of American Express, your Visa or MasterCard will provide the safer option. Most cards these days have charging limits of $5,000 or more. Two cards, then, will provide up to $10,000 in liquid credit. And while the interest rate may be more favorable at the bank, the payments you'll be expected to make on your credit card debts will be quite managable, even if you max the cards out. Most require little more than the interest due each month. Now, while this means the principal might take ten years to pay back, it also means you have three or four months of financing, and the

CREDIT CARD DEBT

Credit card debt can get out of control and can bring about the end of life as we know it. Take, for instance, the case of, well, I'll call him Harry. Harry was a kind man, very supportive of his boss, a small businessman I'll call George. George was in the metalworking business, making ornamental ironwork, and he was good at it. His gates, candlesticks, plant stands, etc., were much in demand, and he sold all he could make at craft shows and for special orders. George was selling all he and his four employees could make, even working six days a week. Unfortunately, machines, steel, welding rods, drill bits, grinding wheels and so on used by metalworkers are even more expensive than those used by their woodworking counterparts, and George was giving his product away. In some instances, he was selling his products for less than it cost to make them. What happened, then, was inevitable: George ran out of money. Bills went unpaid, and his credit went south. Unable to get a bank loan, he turned to his employee and friend, Harry, for help. And Harry gave it. Harry's credit was better than most. He had six or seven high-limit credit cards. With these he paid the outstanding bills, took on the payroll using cash advances on the cards and, while he was running up more than $30,000 worth of debt of his own—business was good, and therefore it must be profitable, or so he thought—George continued giving his product away. The end was a long time coming. George could make only minimum payments on Harry's credit card balances, and the principals continued to grow. Then came the time when he couldn't even make the minimum payments. He had to let Harry and the rest of the crew go, continuing on by himself. Today, George is an old man, still pottering around the workshop, making ornamental ironwork for sale. He has a good income and, thanks to Harry, is debtfree. What happened to Harry? He's still making payments on those debts, and will be for a long time to come. Last I heard, he'd taken a second mortgage on his house to pay off his debts. You see, the debts were his, not George's, and there was nothing he could do about it. Now I know that this is an exceptional case, a horror story, but it's true. Harry was his own worst enemy: Stupid, if you like, but his story illustrates what can happen when credit card debt gets out of control. It also illustrates what happens if you don't do the math. It's easy to make a sale when your price is below cost. Your first priority, then, is to make sure you're selling your goods at a profit. If not, the end, no matter how far in the distance, is inevitable.

pressure that comes with a short-term bank loan will be off—somewhat. Unfortunately, as with any type of loan, if your business is not profitable, credit card debt can get you into a lot of trouble.

Home Equity Loan

This type of financing is a product of the 1990s. If you own your own home and have some equity in it, you can visit a financial institution and realize some, if not all, of that equity. My advice is: Don't do it. I've gone through some tough times in the past, and my home equity—my security blanket, if you like—was something tangible for me to hang on to. But that's not the only reason to avoid this type of financing. Depending on the financial institution involved, the interest rates you'll be required to pay may or may not be favorable, especially if your credit is not as good as it might be. Knowing they have you over a barrel, those institutions that specialize in lending to poor risks often do so because they know they can get a higher rate; you could end up paying back three, even four, times the amount of the original loan. Still, the money's there if you need it. Some off-the-wall institutions will even lend you the difference between your first mortgage and up to 125 percent of the value of your home. One has to wonder why, and what sort of trouble could come with such an arrangement. Again, my advice is this: If you do decide to apply for a home equity loan, go to the bank

where you do business regularly. They will be familiar with you and, as long as there's enough equity available, they should be willing to let you have some seed money. And the interest rate will be in line with national guidelines.

Small Business Loans

These are not as easy to come by as you might think. First, they are rarely small. Many institutions have small business loan guidelines that include minimum numbers, often starting around $50,000. If you're looking for five or ten thousand dollars, you'll be disappointed. Having said that, if you're looking for a sizable chunk of change, the money is usually available—if you qualify—and the interest rates will often be less than those for a regular loan—but you will be expected to jump through hoops to get it.

So how do you qualify? Well, it often can be one of those catch-22 situations: You can get the money only if you don't need it. You will have had to have done most of the work, setting things up, before you will even be considered for such a loan. You will be required to present a sound and thorough business plan to your bank. Yes, the bank makes these loans: The Small Business Administration only guarantees them. What exactly does a business plan involve? There are people that specialize in such plans and, in the first instance, you should go to your accountant for advice and recommendation.

But basically, you will be required to estimate annual income and expenditure, overhead, tooling, pricing structure, customer base, where you'll find new customers, timelines and, of course, profitability. Easy enough you might say. Not so. A business plan can run 10, 20 or even 30 pages and, as a rule, it's not something you can expect to put together without professional help. The cost of such a plan can run into thousands of dollars, which is all you're looking for in the first place.

Financial Backers

This was an opportunity that came my way once. A friend of mine offered to put up the money to expand my business. I turned it down. Borrowing money from friends is *not* a good idea. Within minutes of closing the deal, the one-time friend will turn into a monster who thinks he owns you body and soul. The same goes when borrowing money from members of the family. But that wasn't the main reason I turned him down. To take the loan would have meant that I was under obligation to grow the business, take on staff, expand the customer base and so on. This in order for my backer to realize a profit on his investment. It was something I wasn't prepared to do. You, however, might be. So, how do you find a backer? Networking is probably your best bet. Start with the people you know and, if you think they have the financial resources, ask. If you have no luck there, ask for referrals. People with money tend, like birds of a feather, to flock together, and there are more of them around than you might think. You will, of course, have to be able to present your prospective backer with a sound business plan.

YOU CAN MAKE IT ON YOUR OWN

You really can make it on your own, without going outside for financial help. I did. All it takes is patience and hard work. True, you might have to spend a little longer working for someone else, but so what. If you can start out in business without going into debt, that's the way to do. Peace of mind is worth a great deal. Even if you have little money now, if you have the basic tools—a table saw, a drill motor and one or two basic hand tools—you can get started making the smaller of the ten projects you'll find in this book. That's why they're there. I said previously you can sell your first piece within a week of reading this book, and it's true. I'll go even farther: You can get started within a week and with less than $100. Literally, all you need is a couple of boards, a pot of glue, some screws, a can of stain, a can of finish and the will to win, and you can do it. It's as simple as that. You can self-finance your small business while you're holding down a regular job. Within six months, if you follow the instructions in this book, you can quit that job, if that's what you want to do, and go about your business debt free and with confidence.

chapter eight

PERFECT WOOD FINISHING

There are no secrets here. Two things to remember: A piece of work is only as good—salable—as its finish and, as with construction, finishing should be kept as simple as possible, except when a custom finish has been ordered—and you can charge more for that.

FILLING THE GRAIN

This is a process not widely practiced among amateur woodworkers. It is, however, essential to a professional-looking finish. The surface of an open-grained wood, such as oak, can feel like the mountains of the moon if the filling step is skipped. Go to an outlet and run your fingers over the finish on any piece you choose, and you'll find that the surface is very smooth: The grain has been filled. You can buy proprietary brands of grain filler at most paint stores. I, however, prefer to use the one I learned many years ago in high school. It's quick, inexpensive, doesn't shrink and sands like glass; I'm talking about plaster of Paris. You can find it at most of the large hardware chains in the paint department. A half-gallon bucket will cost about $1.50 and will make enough to do several large pieces of furniture.

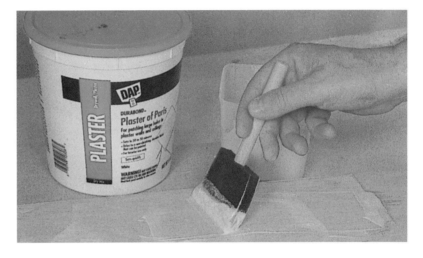

Application

Simply take a small amount of the plaster of Paris powder, place it in a small container, add water and mix until you have a thick, but brushable, paste. Now you'll have to work quickly, because the plaster will begin to set up almost as soon as the mixing is complete. Simply brush the paste all over the surface of the piece you're working on. Watch as you do it, making sure the paste gets into all the crevices. Allow about 30 minutes for the plaster to dry out completely.

Sanding

Once the plaster is completely dry, you can begin sanding it off. Start with a 120 grit on your orbital sander, and keep a hose linked to your dust collector close by.

STEP 1.

Lay the plaster of Paris down as a thick cream, making sure to work it into the grain.

STEP 2.
This is what the surface should look like when the plaster has fully dried—this takes about an hour.

Sand away all the surplus plaster down to the surface of the wood. As you clear it away there will be lots of white dust; be sure your dust collector is running. Finally, finish the sanding with 220-grit paper. The cavities in the grain will now show white against the natural color of the wood; no matter, it will stain perfectly, leaving a completely smooth surface.

FINISH SANDING

This is one stage of the process you can't skimp on. Depending on the type of wood

STEP 3.
This is how the grain should look after sanding. All the pits have been filled and show up white.

used, I start with 80-grit paper and work my way through the grades to 220 grit. The better the piece is sanded, the better the final finish. Much of the sanding must be done before construction is begun: door panels, shelves, legs, rails and stiles and so on. Trying to sand these areas once the piece has been put together wastes time and is grossly inefficient. Do all you can as early in the process as you can.

STAINING

This, too, should be done before assembly. There's nothing more frustrating than to look at a large completed piece knowing that you'll spend the next six or seven hours inside the thing trying to ensure that every little section is properly and completely stained. To do it when all the pieces are ready for assembly makes the whole process quick and simple—and coverage is never a problem.

As to the stain itself, you will need a range of colors, the backbone of which should be what I call *the standards*. I use Minwax brand to maintain standards, and keep the following shades on hand: Provincial, Early American, Golden Oak and Dark Oak. Other shades I buy as I need them.

POLYURETHANE

I use a lot of polyurethane. For my own stuff I use a variety of finishes, but for furniture for sale I stick mostly with the easy application and hard finish polyurethane provides. Again, I use only a top-quality brand. What I lose up front on the cost of the product, I more than gain back in time saved and a high-quality finish. And, as already mentioned, I do occasionally use the new two-in-one stain and polyurethane. Depending on the piece, I use both water- and spirit-based products. The water-based product has some advantages over the spirit-based product, mostly the lack of odor and easy cleanup. You can use whatever suits you best.

Application

For this I use only sponge rubber brushes in various sizes; I do buy these by the case to save money.

I also use Minwax Polyshades: a combination product. I find the idea of staining and finishing in one operation to be a good one. Anything that can be done to cut down on time is good; to cut out a complete finishing step is even better.

SHELLAC/FRENCH POLISH

Shellac is an old-world finish still used today, but rarely applied as it was by the Old Masters. It is, perhaps, the best of sealers, and other finishes can be applied over the top of it. French polishing with shellac as it was done by the Old Masters has almost died away; done properly, however, it is a very exciting finish. To do it right requires dedication and hard work; it's a tedious process, but the results are well worth all the effort.

I use more shellac than varnish, but only on reproduction pieces. For antiquing, I use one of the unrefined shellacs—seedlac or buttonlac—usually mixed at a 3 pound cut. It gives the finished product an old-world look that's hard to beat. For light finishes I use orange shellac.

The Product

You can buy shellac ready mixed as a liquid, usually as a three pound cut, or you can buy the raw flakes and mix it yourself, which is the method I prefer. For reproduction antiques you'll need one of the less refined shellacs, such a seedlac, buttonlac or garnetlac. These need straining before use, but produce a nice range of tones from brown to amber. Orange and blonde shellacs do not need to be strained and, in some cases, you may need to use one of these too.

The Cut

This refers to the mixture: One pound of flakes to one gallon of denatured alcohol is a one pound cut. Of course, you'll never mix a gallon at a time; two ounces to a pint (about 4 tablespoons to 1¼ cups) works nicely as a one pound cut; four ounces (8 tablespoons) per pint makes a two pound cut; six ounces (12 tablespoons) makes a three pound cut and so on.

Method

Mixing: Put the flakes into a glass container—a large jelly jar with a tight-fitting lid will do fine—and then add the alcohol. Put the lid on and allow the mixture to stand for several hours, stirring occasionally, until the flakes are completely dissolved. If you've used one of the shellacs that need straining, pour it through a paint filter, and then return it to the jar; it's now ready to use.

Application

First you'll need to do any necessary staining and distressing.

For Sealing

As a sealer, a one pound cut will do fine. Simply apply a coat with a natural bristle brush, wait for it to dry, about 45 minutes, and then sand lightly.

As a Finish

To use shellac as a finish, a three pound cut is best; it's easier going with two pound, but you'll need to apply more coats. Shellac sets up quite quickly, so you'll have to work fast. Using a natural bristle brush, apply your first coat, allow it to dry, and then sand lightly with 180-grit sandpaper. Apply two or three more coats leaving each one to dry overnight. There is no need to sand between coats. The second coat will dissolve and mix with the first to form a single thick coat, and so on. However, before you apply each subsequent coat, you should inspect the previous one; you may find a run or two. These can be taken off with 180-grit sand-

paper. When you've applied the final coat, and it's dried thoroughly, take a piece of 400-grit wet-and-dry—you might go as fine as 600 grit, if you like—dampen it with linseed oil, and then gently rub the entire surface. Finally, remove the residue of the oil by gently wiping the surface with a soft cloth barely dampened with alcohol. You should now have a finish to be proud of. If you've distressed lightly and used one of the darker shellacs, you'll be amazed at what you've achieved.

French Polishing

This requires a one pound cut and some real dedication on your part. First, sand the piece smooth, do any necessary distressing and apply a nongrain-raising stain of an appropriate color. Then take a soft, lintfree cloth, roll it into a ball and dip it into the shellac. Now rub the shellac onto the wood using fast, straight strokes along the grain. After the first coat has dried, about 45 minutes to an hour, it should be lightly sanded using 600-grit paper. Continue to add coats, lightly sanding between each one, until the finish begins to glow. Now add 8 to 10 drops of boiled linseed oil to the shellac, mix well and apply another coat, this time rubbing in a circular motion. Continue to add more coats, adding a little more oil to the shellac with each one, until a deep, glowing finish is achieved. You'll need to apply at least 8 coats, and perhaps as many as a dozen or even more.

PAINTED FINISHES

Most Early American and English everyday furniture, especially that used in kitchens or family rooms, was painted for a number of reasons: To protect and beautify it, to match the overall decor of a room or to make an inexpensive wood look like another (grain painting). And at some time in the future, you may want to reproduce some of these finishes. If so, you can refer to my book *Building Classic Antique Furniture With Pine* (Popular Woodworking Books, 1997), where you'll find the processes for antique finishes laid out in detail.

Today, the painted finish is enjoying something of a comeback. Large pieces and small pieces can be found partly or completely painted in a variety of muted colors: hunter green, barn red, country blue and so on. These colors are easy enough to apply, as long as you stick with water-based paints.

APPLICATORS FOR PAINTS

First, you should remember that all old painted finishes were applied by hand, often by someone who wasn't too bothered about a professional look. This means brushmarks, and there would have been runs here and there. Today, paint is applied quickly with spraying equipment. If you own such equipment, fine. If not, as long as you stick with water-based paints, this is not a problem.

Many people say you can't do a decent paint job unless you spray. Not true. I apply everything with a brush, even stains. You, however, should use whichever method you feel most comfortable with. I own a half-dozen expensive bristle and nylon brushes, and I buy foam/poly brushes by the case. I use natural bristle brushes for oil-based paints, and synthetic bristles for latex and acrylic mediums. This is because water causes natural bristles to swell. Use a good brush, and you can lay the paint down very nicely—better, I think, than you can with a spray gun; thicker, for sure. Even so, you'll find the piece will often need at least two coats to cover properly, especially when using dark colors. A good brush is an investment; a cheap brush is an expense.

What's a good brush? Apart from it costing $30 to $40, the bristles on a good brush, natural or synthetic, should all be tapered and "flagged" (split at the tips to form tiny forks). Even on the best brushes, however, all the bristles may not be split, but the more that are, the better. Hold the brush up to the light and separate the bristles: You should be able to see the splits. Compare several brushes; you'll find one may have more flags than another. That's the one you want. The bristles should also have a definite spring to them, and they should taper to a chisel edge at the tip. Start out with a 3″ brush. It will do most jobs, and you can add other sizes as your budget allows.

PRICING STRATEGIES

A lot has been written on the subject of pricing, volumes in fact, and I'm not going into it in great depth here. I will, however, give you the method I use. It may not be the best; it's certainly controversial, but it's simple and works well enough for me. It's based on the cost of the principal material used to make the product: wood.

I used to price my work the conventional way, which, in simple terms, is to first establish an hourly labor rate, determine the cost of overhead, factor in the cost of all the material down to the last nail and screw, hidden overheads such as insurance, medical expenses, etc., and then add it all up and add a percentage for profit. Unfortunately, when using conventional methods to establish the cost of labor, the price for the finished product was always too high, and not just by a little. Sometimes the price was more than double what my potential buyers were willing to pay. This system might work well enough if you're selling only retail, but for the trade, no. I spent a lot of time figuring out the method described below. A lot of trial and error went into it. Today, I have refined it to the point where I can quickly figure out a price for a given piece in my head if I have to—a situation you should avoid if you can—knowing my profit is secure.

A word of warning is appropriate here: It's not a good idea to sell to individuals at the same prices you sell to the trade, especially if the trade is your main source of income. No buyer wants a supplier to be a direct competitor. Either choose your battleground, trade or retail, and stick to it, or increase your prices when you sell direct to the public. If you don't, and your trade customers find out that you're undermining them, you'll lose them.

METHOD

For a wholesale situation—to price for the trade—simply calculate the cost of the wood used in the product, add 10 percent to allow for wastage, and then multiply the total by either 5, 4 or 3: For woods costing around $1 to $2 per board foot, round up to the nearest dollar and multiply by 5; for wood costing $2 to $4 per board foot, round up to the nearest dollar and multiply the total by 4; for wood costing in excess of $4 per board foot, round up to the nearest dollar and then multiply by 3.

If you're selling direct to the public, calculate the price for the piece as described above and then add 50 percent. You can vary the percentage if you like, a little less for larger pieces, perhaps, but only in special cases. Your retail price will almost always be competitive, especially when you take into account the quality you're offering.

Simplistic?

Now I know this may seem to be oversimplistic, at least compared to the other methods of pricing that take into account all sorts of factors to extract the last cent of profit. But my method works—and it works well. I make good money, and I'm always sure I'm making a profit. Maybe I could make more, but I think not. This is a very competitive business, and whenever I up my prices, I price myself out of the market. Doing it this way I've never lost money. The method even allows for extra labor, if the time should come when you need it. And from time to time, you will.

If you would like to get into pricing in detail, I recommend you purchase *The Woodworker's Guide to Pricing Your Work* by Dan Ramsey (Betterway Books; $18.95).

QUICK REFERENCE GUIDE TO PRICING

To give you a quick reference guide when pricing your products, the following sections describe a stripped-down version of the pricing for each piece covered in the project section. This is exactly the way I do it; it should work well for you too, but feel free to adjust com-

ponents up or down to suit your own specific market conditions.

Shelving: Version 1

2.5 board feet of oak at $1.20—round that up to $2. Multiply 2.5 by $2.00 = material cost of $5. Multiply $5 by 5 = $25; add 10% ($2.50) to cover wastage = selling price of $27.50.

Shelving: Version 2

4 board feet of oak at $1.20—round that up to $2. Multiply 4 by $2.00 = material cost of $8. Add 10% ($.80) to cover wastage = $8.80. Multiply $8.80 by 5 = selling price of $44.00.

Blanket Chest

30 board feet of furniture-grade pine at 65 cents—round that up to $1.00. Multiply 30 by $1.00 = material cost of $30. Add 10% ($3.00) to cover wastage = $33.00. Multiply $33.00 by 5 = selling price of $165.00.

Dining Table

23 board feet of oak at $1.20—round that up to $2.00. Multiply 23 by $2.00 = material cost of $46. Add 10% ($4.60) to cover wastage = $50.60. Multiply $50.60 by 5 = selling price of $253.00.

Bathroom Cabinet

22 board feet of furniture-grade pine at 65 cents—round that up to $1.00. Multiply 22 by $1.00 = material cost of $22. Add 10%

($2.20) to cover wastage = $24.20. Multiply $24.20 by 5 = selling price of $121.00.

Jelly Cabinet

30 board feet of furniture-grade pine at 65 cents—round that up to $1.00. Multiply 30 by $1.00 = material cost of $30. Add 10% ($3.00) to cover wastage = $33.00. Multiply $33.00 by 5 = selling price of $165.00.

Country Bookcase

27 board feet of furniture-grade pine at 65 cents—round that up to $1.00. Multiply 27 by $1.00 = material cost of $27. Add 10% ($2.70) to cover wastage = $29.70. Multiply $29.70 by 5 = selling price of $148.50.

Veggie Bin

11 board feet of furniture-grade pine at 65 cents—round that up to $1.00. Multiply 11 by $1.00 = material cost of $11. Add 10% ($1.10) to cover wastage = $11.10. Multiply $11.10 by 5 = selling price of $60.50.

Sofa Table

10 board feet of oak at $1.20—round that up to $2.00. Multiply 10 by $2.00 = $20.00. Add four legs at $2.00 each = $28.00. Add 10% ($2.80) to cover wastage = $30.80. Multiply $30.80 by 5 = selling price of $154.00.

Computer Desk

26 board feet oak at $1.20—round that up to $2.00. Multiply 26 by $2.00 = material cost of $52.00. Add 10% ($5.20) to cover wastage = $57.20. Multiply $57.20 by 5 = selling price of $286.00.

Entertainment Center

40 board feet oak at $1.20—round that up to $2.00. Multiply 40 by $2.00 = $80.00. Add 14 board feet furniture-grade pine at 65 cents, rounded up to $1.00 = $94.00. Add 10% ($9.40) to cover wastage = total material cost of $103.40. Multiply $103.40 by 5 = selling price of $517.00.

TEN PROJECTS THAT WILL MAKE YOU MONEY

Now to the good stuff. The ten projects in this section of the book have been included for several reasons, the first of which is their sales appeal. Each piece is a member of my own top ten best-selling products. Each has sold many times, some more than 100 times. They all have a universal appeal, and thus should sell anywhere.

The second reason they have been included is that, for the most part, they are all fairly simple to make, even the large pieces. The smaller pieces also lend themselves well to small-scale mass production: You can make 5, 10 or even 20 all at the same time. This means you'll save time, and thus money, in many areas of the construction process: cutting, staining and even assembly. You can set stops on your machines and cut 20 sets of components almost as quickly as you can cut 1 set using conventional measuring and marking methods. By the same token, it's just as easy to stain a large number of components as it is 2 or 3.

Third, they have been chosen to give you some variety. You have one or two extremely simple, although easy to sell, products at the one end, and a couple of fairly sophisticated pieces at the other. If you want to concentrate on the quick and easy, fine—you can make a nice living, and certainly some handy extra cash, doing just that. If you want to go for the more prestigious pieces, you can do that too.

Fourth, each of the ten has an aesthetic appeal all its own: They look nice. This in itself makes them extremely salable.

As to the materials: All of the pieces can be made in variety of woods. I have chosen pine and oak for two reasons. Pine is inexpensive, easy to work and finish, and is extremely popular with the buying public. Oak, especially red oak, is also inexpensive and, while it's not as easy to work, it is easy to finish and looks great as well; it, too, is very popular with the buying public. Any and all of the pieces could be made from cherry, walnut or maple, but, as mentioned previously, the cost of the stock lumber, if not prohibitive, makes mistakes very expensive. So, at least during the early days, I suggest you stick with pine and oak.

There are, of course, many more pieces in my portfolio, but these are the ones I think you'll do best with. What I am sure of is this: If you follow the steps I've laid out in this book, and make a professional job of the projects, you will make money making furniture, and you'll begin doing it just as soon as you've completed the first one or two projects.

Shelving

Everybody needs shelving, even the most affluent home, the most distinguished museum or library, even Ivy League universities, not to mention the average American family with 2.4 kids and a couple of cars. Shelves sell well. They are a ready and easy source of income, and ideal for someone new to making money making furniture. There are many, many versions of the lowly shelf you can make, and for each and every one there's a market ready and waiting. I've included two here. Both have made me a lot of money and, with various

changes and adjustments, you could make a very nice living doing nothing else. The first is nothing more than a standard 36″ × 6″ shelf with a couple of supports; you can make it from oak or pine. Oak has more appeal and opens up the market to include oak furniture outlets. The second piece is more complex and is as much a plate rack as it is a set of shelves, designed for the collector of bric-a-brac. This one could be made of pine, but experience leads me to tell you that it should be made from oak so that it can be stained and coated with polyurethane. I've sold literally hundreds of the first version, and almost as many of the other.

CONSTRUCTION NOTES

Both shelves are made from #1 common red oak. The first version is a simple shelf with a couple of shaped supports, drilled and counterbored to take the screws used to fasten it to the wall. You can change the length to suit your client's needs. The other version is a multishelved affair incorporating plate grooves and some decorative detail. The shelves and top are fastened to the sides with through dado joints. You'll be able to make several of each version during the course of a single day.

CONSTRUCTION DETAILS
Version 1

This is a very simple piece to make. If you only make one, it will take you less than an

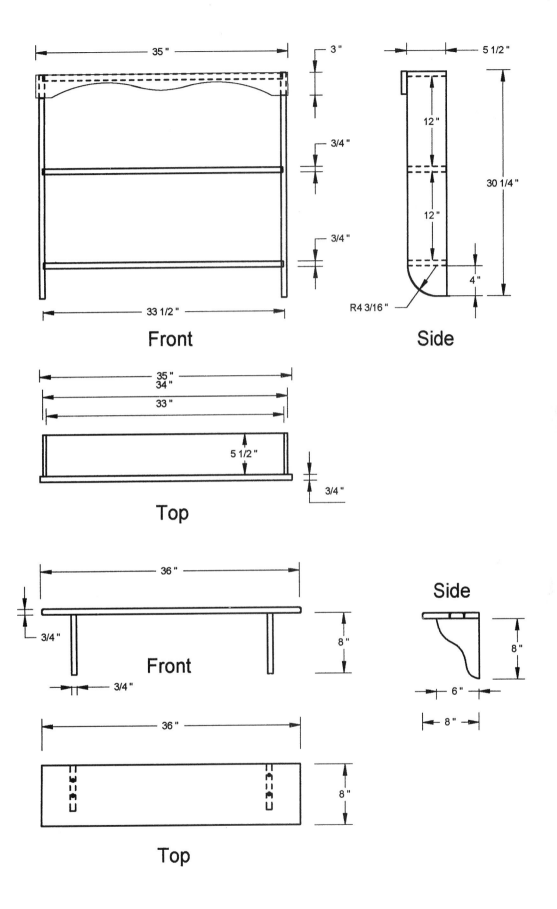

Front

Side

Top

Front

Side

Top

To cut the plate groove, set the router table fence about 2″ away from the center point, mark the start and finish points on your router table fence, align the end of the shelf with the starting point, and then gently plunge the upper face of the shelf down onto the bit and run it through to the finish point.

hour from start to finish. If you make a dozen, small-time production methods will allow you to complete them twice as fast.

STEP 1. Cut the board that will form the shelf to length and width.

STEP 2. Run it through the jointer to clean up the edges.

STEP 3. Bore four holes to take the screws that will fasten the shelf to the supports and counterbore them.

STEP 4. Sand the surfaces to a fine finish with 220 grit.

STEP 5. Ease all four edges to remove the corners.

STEP 6. From a piece of stock 8″ square, cut the supports to the pattern shown in the drawing; you can use either a band saw or a jigsaw for this.

STEP 7. Sand the supports smooth, and ease the edges as you did for the shelf board.

STEP 8. If you are using red oak, use plaster of Paris or the proprietary brand of your choice and fill the grain on all three pieces, and then set them aside to allow the filler to dry completely.

STEP 9. Once the filler has dried, sand away the surplus and finish sand all three pieces to 320 grit.

STEP 10. Using 2″ × #10 screws, assemble the supports to the shelf.

STEP 11. Plug the holes and sand the plugs smooth.

STEP 12. Stain the completed assembly.

STEP 13. Protect the finished piece with a couple of coats of polyurethane.

Version 2

This version is also quite simple to construct. If you only make one, you should have no trouble completing it, start to finish, in less than two hours. I can make six of them in a production run in less than six hours.

STEP 1. Cut all the pieces to size, thickness-plane them to ¾″, joint the edges and sand them smooth to 220 grit.

STEP 2. Use either a band saw or a jigsaw to cut the detail on the bottom ends of the two sides and on the top trim, as shown in the drawing.

STEP 3. Set your dado blade to cut at ¾″ wide, assemble it into your table saw, and then set the depth of cut to ¼″. If you prefer, you can use a router, a dado jig and a ¾″ bit set to cut ¼″ deep.

STEP 4. Mill the dadoes and rabbets to the sides as shown in the drawing. Use a sacrifice rip fence for the rabbets or, if your fence allows it, you can pull it back and use it as a depth stop as shown in the photograph.

STEP 5. Assemble either a v-groove or a ¼″ roundnose bit into your router table.

STEP 6. Set your router table fence 2½″ back from the center of the bit.

STEP 7. Set the bit to cut to a depth of ⅜″.

STEP 8. Apply masking tape to the fence to

Use your band saw to cut out the shelf supports.

act as a measuring guide, as shown in the photograph.

STEP 9. Mark the tape 2″ in both directions from the center of the bit. Now you're ready to cut the plate grooves.

STEP 10. Take one of the shelf boards and, using the marks on the masking tape as your guide, slowly plunge the board down onto the bit. Run the board against the back fence until the other end reaches the second mark, and then

carefully lift and remove the piece from the table.

STEP 11. Repeat the process for the second shelf.

STEP 12. Glue and assemble the two shelves and the top to the two sides, making sure the plate grooves are facing up and are at the rear, clamp the assembly, and then check the diagonals to ensure all is square. If necessary, make any adjustments, and then set the assembly aside

Sand the edge of the shelf supports on your oscillating spindle sander. You can also use the front edge of your belt sander for this operation.

and allow the glue to fully cure, preferably overnight.

STEP 13. When the glue has fully cured, remove the clamps and assemble the top trim to the outer edge of the top. You can use finishing nails for this step, if you like. Be sure to fill the holes and sand them smooth.

STEP 14. Clean up and wipe the assembly with 320-grit paper.

STEP 15. Stain the piece, and then apply a couple of coats of polyurethane for protection.

PRICING

Using our trusty formula, you'll find the first shelf will sell for a very reasonable price. There are 2.5 board feet of red oak in the piece at a cost of $1.20 per board foot. Round that up to $2, and you have a ma-

Toenail screws to the underside of the shelf/dado joints. This will strengthen the joints.

terial cost of $5. Multiplying that by 5 gives you $25; add 10 percent to cover wastage, and you have a sale price of $27.50.

The second version has a total of 4 board feet of red oak, which will give you a base of $8×5 for $40. Add 10 percent, and you have a sale price of $44.

THE MARKETS

You can sell these pieces just about anywhere: country stores, craft shows, flea markets, oak furniture outlets and even fine furniture stores. As I've already mentioned, you can make a good living just making shelves. They are easy to find in country outlets, but oak outlets and fine furniture stores have a difficult time obtaining them; large manufacturers can't be bothered with them. If you want to make some real money making shelves, visit every furniture store within a 50 mile radius of your shop. You'll soon have more orders than you can handle: Don't be afraid to quote prices for custom versions.

MATERIALS

VERSION ONE

Sides:

30¼″×5½″	2 pieces

Shelves

33″×5½″	2 pieces

Top

33″×5½″	1 piece

Top Trim

35″×3″	1 piece

VERSION TWO

Shelf

36″×8″	1 piece

Supports

8″×6″	2 pieces

Blanket Chest

This is a good old standby. Blanket chests have always been popular. You'll find them in every type of furniture store. Most have cedar linings, but many people don't like the smell. This is a popular version and size. You can make it from pine, from oak or from any hardwood. I've made this one from pine.

Use your jointer to true up all edges before gluing up the panels for the top and sides.

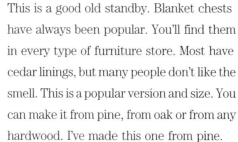

CONSTRUCTION OUTLINE

The piece is constructed from furniture-grade pine at a moisture content of less than 10 percent. This is particularly important for two reasons: First, the material is inexpensive compared to the more exotic hardwoods, and second, it is much more stable than shelving-board pine, considering the large areas of board involved. You could, of course, make it from oak, but you would end up with a piece that might be too expensive to sell; stick with pine. All of the large boards are built using butt joints and biscuits. The box sides and ends are assembled together using dovetail joints. Again, for two reasons: first, the joint is very strong and the assembly will never break apart, and second, the finished product will look wonderful. You'll rarely find a commercially made chest with dovetail construction, and even if you do, it will be at a price far higher than yours. Do a professional job of the construction, and especially the finish, and you'll have a very desirable piece of furniture.

CONSTRUCTION NOTES

STEP 1. Cut all the parts roughly to size and joint the edges.

STEP 2. Build the six boards that will make the front, back, ends, bottom and lid of the upper chest.

STEP 3. When the glue has cured, sand all the boards smooth to 120 grit.

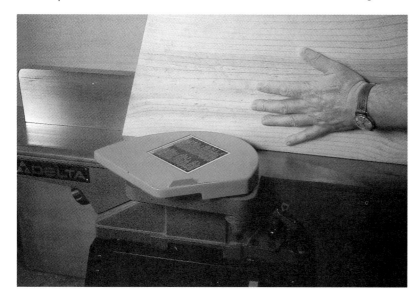

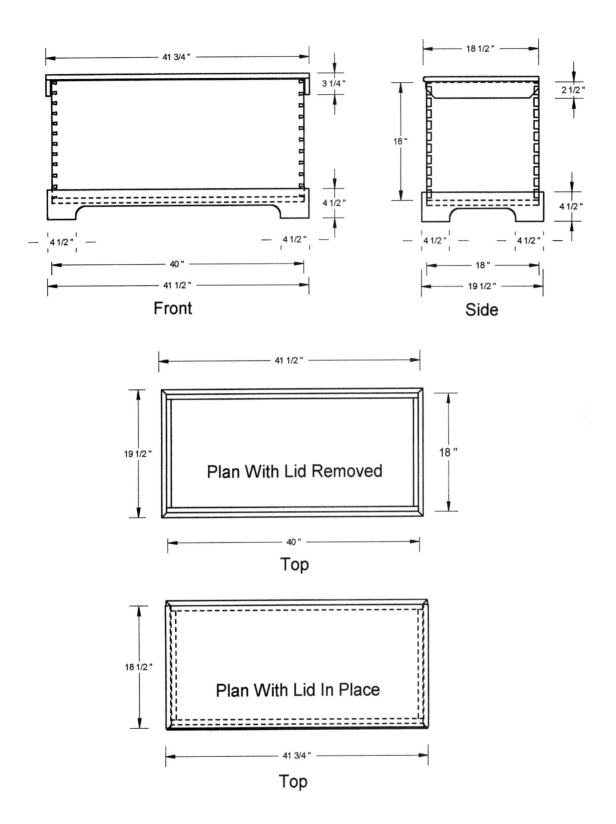

Front

Side

Plan With Lid Removed

Top

Plan With Lid In Place

Top

Make sure that your bit cuts the line that indicates the depth of the joint exactly in half. This will eliminate lots of problems during assembly and finishing: If you cut above the line, you'll have to fill the joints or sand away the boards themselves; if you cut below the line, you'll have to sand away the pins and tails.

To ensure your dovetails are true and tight, make sure the top edge of the board touches all of the jig's fingers, and that the side edge of the board touches both of the left-hand stops.

STEP 4. If you have a dovetail jig—I use Leigh's—turn the guide fingers to the TD mode and set the fingers at roughly 2½" intervals. This configuration provides a pleasing effect.

STEP 5. Turn the guide fingers over and cut the tails to the front and back boards of the chest.

STEP 6. Turn the guide fingers back to the TD mode, set the assembly to cut the pins slightly oversize, and cut the pins to the edge of one of the ends.

STEP 7. Remove the workpiece from the jig and test the fit to either the front or back of the upper chest. The fit should be tight. If the pins are too large, reset the jig, replace the workpiece in the jig,

and re-cut the pins. Be sure you don't cut them too small.

STEP 8. When you've re-cut the pins, test the fit once again. If you have it right, cut the remaining pins.

STEP 9. Glue. Make sure you use plenty of glue when you assemble the dovetailed sections; I use yellow carpenter's glue. Glue, assemble and clamp. Check the diagonals to make sure the box is perfectly square, and then set it aside to cure overnight.

STEP 10. Turn the box so that the bottom edge is uppermost and place it on the bench. Set the bottom board in place, making sure it is flush all around. Now, using ten #6 × 1¾" screws—four along each side and one at each end—fasten the bottom

If you intend to use biscuits to strengthen your butt joints, they should be set 6" to 10" apart.

board to the chest walls, and then turn the chest upright on the bench.

STEP 11. Using the pattern, cut the detail for all four sections of the feet.

STEP 12. Cut the feet sections accurately to length and miter the ends to 45°.

STEP 13. From the inside of the chest, screw the front and rear feet sections in place.

STEP 14. From the inside, and using a little glue on the miters, screw the two end feet sections in place. Set the assembly aside and leave it overnight (or until the glue fully cures).

STEP 15. Mark the cleats and the lid for biscuit slots.

STEP 16. Mill the biscuit slots to the cleats and lid.

STEP 17. Glue and clamp the cleats to the lid. Set the assembly aside and leave it overnight to cure.

STEP 18. Finish-sand the entire assembly using 220-grit paper, but do not attach the lid to the chest yet. Wait until the finishing is complete.

MATERIALS

Lid
One 41¾″ × 18½″
Two 18¼″ × 2½″ cleats

Chest
Two 40″ × 18″
Two 18″ × 18″
One 40″ × 18″ (bottom)
Two 42½″ × 4½″ (front and rear feet—allows extra for miters)
Two 20½″ × 4½″ (end feet—allows extra for miters)

Hardware
Three 3″ decorative hinges
One lid support

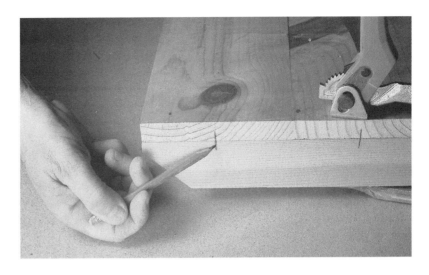

STEP 20. Apply stain to the chest inside and out, and to both sides of the lid.

STEP 21. Apply two coats of satin polyurethane for protection.

STEP 22. Using three hinges, attach the lid to the chest.

STEP 23. Assemble the lid support on the inside of the chest and lid.

PRICING

There are roughly 30 board feet of furniture-grade pine in this piece. I pay 65 cents per foot for mine; you may pay more or less for yours. Using my numbers, round the 65 cents up to $1.00 and multiply that by 30 board feet for a total of $30, add 10 percent to allow for wastage and multiply the result, $33, by 5 for a selling price of $165; a bargain almost anywhere. Chests like this routinely sell in furniture stores for $250 and up.

THE MARKETS

You can sell these chests almost everywhere; even oak outlets will buy pine chests for resale. Just be sure that you do the best possible job on the construction and the finish. If it looks good, it will sell.

To join the cleat to the underside of the lid, mark for biscuits 4″ to 6″ apart. Make sure you mill the joint only where the pencil mark passes over the edge of the board.

Oak Dining Table

This is a timeless piece. Its roots lie deep in the Arts and Crafts movement of the turn of the twentieth century, with such notable designers as Gustav Stickley, William Morris and Gordon Russell. It's as popular a piece today as the original was back in the 1920s. I have one just like it in my dining room. It sells well and is quick, about six to eight hours, and profitable to make. You could, of course, adjust the size up or down according to your client's custom requirements: Smaller it would make a nice end table or coffee table; larger, it could be a dining table to seat more people. Adjust the width to make it narrower and you have a nice library table, desk or refectory table. The possibilities are endless.

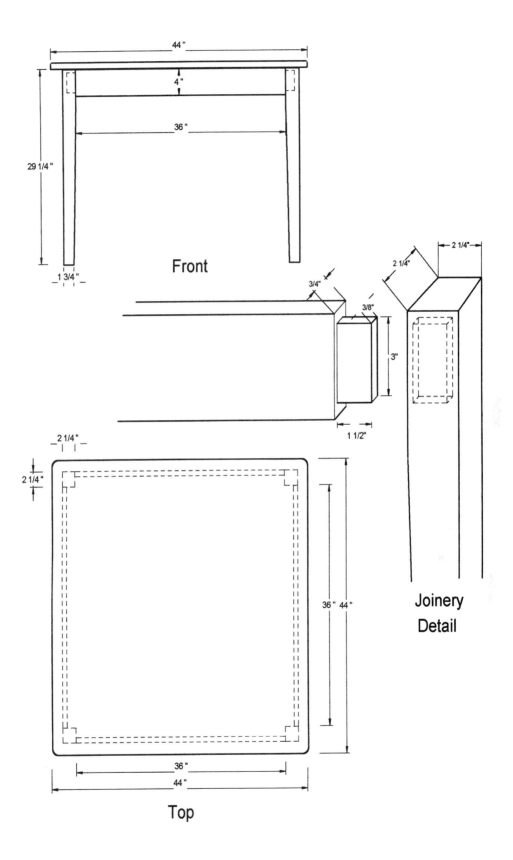

44 "

4 "

36 "

29 1/4 "

1 3/4 "

Front

3/4"

3/8"

3"

2 1/4"

2 1/4"

1 1/2"

Joinery
Detail

2 1/4"

2 1/4"

36 " 44 "

36 "

44 "

Top

It's a good idea to run a piece of masking tape along the back fence of your dedicated mortising machine, and then to mark the start and finish points to ensure each mortise is exactly the same length.

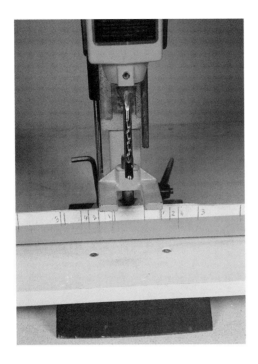

CONSTRUCTION NOTES

This is a fairly simple, straightforward piece to make. The top is constructed from red oak boards a full 1″ thick; the legs are cut from 10/4 unfinished stock; and the apron is made from 4/4 stock finished to ¾″. The legs are tapered on the table saw using a contemporary steel jig—a homemade version would work just as well—and the apron and legs are joined together with mortise-and-tenon joints. The top is fastened to the apron using a little device I designed myself: I make buttons using scrap stock and #20 biscuits (more about that later).

CONSTRUCTION DETAILS
Table Top

STEP 1. Select the boards you'll use to make the top. These should be at least 1¼″ thick.

STEP 2. Cut all the pieces roughly to length: 44¼″.

STEP 3. If you're using rough stock, plane all

of the pieces to the finished thickness of 1″.

STEP 4. Joint all the edges ready for joining.

STEP 5. Lay out the boards ready for marking and joining; be sure to alternate the end grains to minimize future warping.

STEP 6. Mark the pieces for biscuits—each mark should be 9″ to 10″ apart—and make witness marks as shown in the photographs to ensure the pieces go back together in the correct order.

STEP 7. Glue, assemble and clamp the top boards together in two sections, each incorporating half the number of boards needed to complete the top.

STEP 8. Set the two sections aside and allow the glue to fully cure, overnight if at all possible.

STEP 9. When the glue has fully cured, complete the assembly of the tabletop by removing the clamps from the two top sections. Glue the two meeting edges, assemble the two sections, and then clamp them and set them aside until the glue has fully cured.

STEP 10. When the glue has fully cured, remove the clamps and sand the top smooth using 80-grit paper first, and then 120-grit paper.

STEP 11. Using a 7¼″ circular saw and a straightedge, trim the two long edges to their finished length.

STEP 12. Mark a 1″ radius on each of the four corners.

STEP 13. Use a belt sander to round the corners to the radius marks.

STEP 14. Using a ⅜″ roundover bit in your handheld router, round over the upper edge of the top.

STEP 15. Finish-sand the top surface and edges to 220 grit.

Begin at the starting point (1) and finish at point (5) for a mortise that's exactly 3″ long.

STEP 16. Use a creamy mixture of plaster of Paris to fill the grain—be sure to cover the end grains—and set the top aside to allow the plaster to fully cure, at least an hour.

STEP 17. When the plaster has completely dried, sand away the surplus plaster to leave the wood exposed and the grain showing white.

STEP 18. Sand the top to its final finish using 320-grit paper.

STEP 19. Finally, treat the top with your chosen shade of stain and set it aside until you're ready to assemble it to the subframe.

Legs

STEP 1. Cut your stock to make four pieces 29″ long by roughly 2⅜″ square.

STEP 2. Run all four pieces through the jointer to square them to the finished dimensions of 2¼″ square.

STEP 3. Mark the mortises as shown in the drawing.

STEP 4. If you have a dedicated mortising machine, mill all the mortises as shown in the drawing. If you don't have a dedicated machine, cut the mortises by hand.

STEP 5. After you've cut the mortises, measure 5″ from the top end of each leg and make a mark for the start of the taper.

STEP 6. Set your tapering jig to an angle of 1½°.

STEP 7. Raise the table saw blade to its fullest extension; be sure you keep the blade guard in place.

STEP 8. Using the marked leg and your tapering jig, set the rip fence so the blade just touches the mark that indicates the beginning of the taper.

STEP 9. Remove the leg blank from the blade, turn on the saw, and then carefully cut the tapers to two adjacent sides on each of the four legs: The two tapered sides will face inward on the finished table.

STEP 10. Sand the outer surfaces of all four

The best tool for accurately cutting tenons is a professional tenoning jig. This one made by *Delta* can be infinitely adjusted for depth, angle and tilt to ensure the best possible fit.

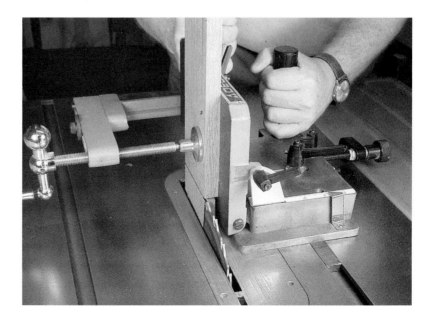

When you are making the button retainers for the top, use a long piece of stock about 2½″ wide. Mill the slot and then cut that section off. Mill another slot, cut that one off and continue this process until you have all your retainers cut.

legs smooth, and then fill the grain and finish the sanding to 320 grit.

Apron

STEP 1. Cut all four pieces roughly to width and length.

STEP 2. Joint the edges.

STEP 3. Trim the ends square and to length.

STEP 4. Use your tenoning jig to mill the tenons as shown in the drawing.

STEP 5. Sand the surfaces to 120 grit.

STEP 6. Fill the grain and allow the plaster to fully cure.

STEP 7. Sand away the surplus plaster of Paris to reveal the surface of the wood and the grain.

STEP 8. Finish-sand the surfaces to 320 grit.

Button Retainers

STEP 1. From scrap oak stock, cut ten pieces 2½″ square by ¾″ thick.

STEP 2. Mill a #20 biscuit slot in one end grain of each piece, just as you would

if you were going to butt joint the pieces.

STEP 3. Drill a ⅛″ hole through the center of each piece, and set all ten pieces aside until you're ready to use them.

Staining

STEP 1. Do any final sanding necessary on all of the pieces.

STEP 2. Using your chosen shade, stain all of pieces and set them aside until they are dry.

Assembly

STEP 1. Using one of the new polyurethane glues, assemble one of the rails that will form the apron to two of the legs, clamp it and set it aside until the glue is fully cured.

STEP 2. Repeat the process with the other two legs.

STEP 3. When the glue in the first two sections of the substructure has fully cured, continue the assembly using the two remaining pieces of the apron.

The finished button retainer with the biscuit in place should look like this.

STEP 4. Clamp the substructure and stand it on its legs, and then measure the diagonal across the top to ensure the assembly is perfectly square. If it isn't, adjust the clamps and clamping pressure to pull it square.

STEP 5. When the glue to the substructure has fully cured, remove the clamps and prepare to attach it to the top.

STEP 6. Using your biscuit jointer, mill ten slots to the top inside edges of the apron: four along two opposing sides, and one to the center of each of the other two opposing sides. It doesn't matter exactly where you position the slots, as long as they're roughly equidistant from each other.

STEP 7. Place the top upside down on the bench; be sure to cover the bench with a soft pad of some sort to protect the finish.

STEP 8. Place the substructure in place on the underside of the top; measure the surrounding lips to ensure it's in the center.

STEP 9. Now take the ten 2½″ square retaining buttons, dry-fit a #20 biscuit to each one, and then slide them into the slots in the edges of the substructure. *Do not use any glue.* The top must be able to move as it swells and contracts.

STEP 10. Using 1¼″ × #10 screws to fasten the biscuits, and thus the substructure, to the top.

Finishing

STEP 1. Wipe the outer surfaces with 320-grit sandpaper.

MATERIALS

Top
44″ × 44″   1 piece

Apron
39″ × 4″   4 pieces

Legs
29¼″ × 2¼″ × 2¼″   4 pieces

Buttons
2½″ × 2½″ × ¾″   10 pieces

STEP 2. Apply two coats of clear, spirit-based polyurethane.

PRICING

Going with the pricing formula: There are roughly 19 board feet of #1 common red oak, plus the legs, in this project. My cost for the regular stock was $1.20 per board foot, and $1.80 per board foot for the legs. This computes to about 23 board feet; adding 10 percent for wastage gives 25 board feet, and with the cost rounded up to $2.00, a total wood cost of $50. Multiply this by 5 and you have a selling price of $250; you can adjust this up or down slightly if you like. Your gross profit before labor costs and other odds and ends is $200. I can make one of these, start to finish, in less than eight hours. Say incidental costs—stain, sanding materials, polyurethane, etc.—run $10, you're left with around $190 for labor and profit. Not bad.

THE MARKETS

This piece will sell readily to oak factory outlets, to country stores and, as long as you've done a professional job of finishing the piece, to fine furniture stores as well.

Bathroom Cabinet

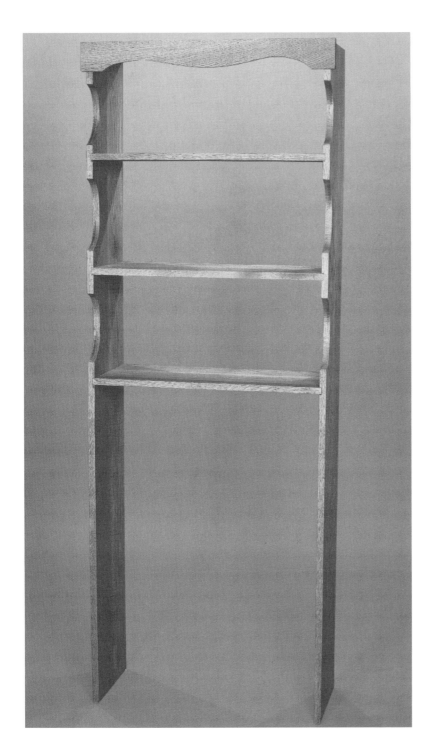

This is a very simple piece to make, but don't let its simplicity fool you. I have sold countless numbers of this item. Rarely a day goes by that I don't get at least one order for the mighty over-commode cabinet. It fulfills two purposes: One, it fills that awkward space over the commode with a nice-looking piece of furniture, and two, it's fully functional, providing lots of storage space for towels and soaps, and even for photographs, pictures and ornaments. This is another one of those pieces that could, in and of itself, provide you with a good living.

CONSTRUCTION OUTLINE

As I've already mentioned, this is a very simple piece to make. I can make one, start to finish, in a couple of hours, and a half dozen on a good day employing mini-assembly-line techniques. For materials, you can use just about anything you like. To keep the price down, use furniture-grade pine; for a classic look, use oak; for a really expensive piece, you could go with a finely finished maple or even walnut. There are a number of ways you could change the design to suit custom orders: You could put a couple of solid doors over the center-shelf space or glass doors over the entire front, or you could take away or add shelves. The construction of the shelves to the sides is no more than

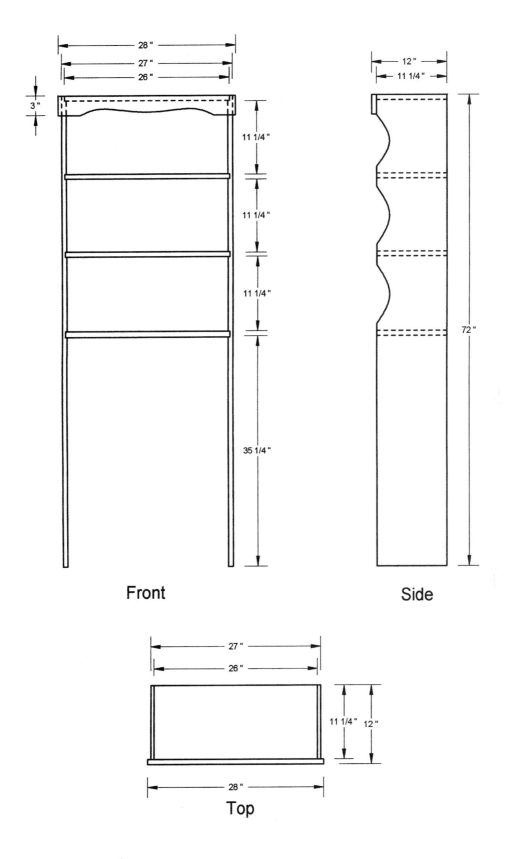

Front

Side

Top

You can speed things up during construction by adding stops to your machines when doing repetitive cuts.

through dado joints; what little trim there is is fastened to the sides and top with glue and biscuits. The cabinet in the photo is made from oak finished with Golden Oak Polyshades; simply wipe it and you're done.

CONSTRUCTION NOTES

STEP 1. Start by cutting all the pieces to size and jointing the edges.

STEP 2. Mark the sides for the position of the shelves, as shown out in the drawing.

On larger pieces it's easier to use a router and mortising bit to mill your dadoes.

STEP 3. Mark the cutout details for the two sides and the trim as shown in the drawing.

STEP 4. Use either a staked dado blade in your table saw or your router and a ¾″ mortising bit to mill the dadoes and rabbets to receive the shelves and top in the two sides.

STEP 5. Use a jigsaw to cut out the details for the two sides.

STEP 6. Use a band saw to cut out the details of the trim.

STEP 7. Sand the trim, sides and shelves smooth with 220-grit paper.

STEP 8. Break all the sharp edges with 120-grit and then 220-grit sandpaper.

STEP 9. If you're using oak, fill the grain using either a proprietary brand of grain filler or plaster of Paris and allow the filler to cure completely.

STEP 10. Once the filler has fully cured, sand the sides and shelves smooth to at least 220 grit.

STEP 11. If you intend to use stain, now's the time to do it. If you're using a stain-poly finish combination, you can leave this step until the assembly is finished.

STEP 12. Now, using a good quality glue, assemble the shelves and top to the sides, clamp it and then measure the diagonals to ensure the structure is square.

STEP 13. Make any adjustments necessary to square the piece and then, using #6 × 1¾″ drywall screws from the underside, toenail the shelves to the sides for added strength.

STEP 14. Measure the diagonals again to ensure the structure is square, and then set it aside to allow the glue to fully cure.

STEP 15. When the glue has fully cured, remove the clamps and lay the structure on the floor, sunny-side up—the front facing upward.

STEP 16. Now lay the trim in the appropriate place and mark for biscuit slots.

STEP 17. Mill the biscuit slots to the trim and top.

STEP 18. Glue, assemble and clamp the trim to the top, making sure all of the joints are tight, with no gaps between them. Set the structure aside until the glue has fully cured.

STEP 19. When the glue has fully cured, remove the clamps, clean away any excess glue and finish-sand the entire piece to at least 220 grit—320 is even better, especially if you're using oak.

STEP 20. If you intend to use a stain-poly combination finish, now's the time to do it. Just wipe it on and let it dry completely.

STEP 21. If the surface feels like it might need a final rub with 320-grit paper, you can do so, and then apply a final coat of finish. Bear in mind, however, that a second coat of stain-poly will darken the color slightly.

STEP 22. If you stained the pieces before assembly, apply a couple of coats of satin polyurethane for protection.

MATERIALS

Sides:

72″×11¼″   2 pieces

Shelves:

26″×11¼″   3 pieces

Top

26″×11¼″   1 piece

Trim:

3½″×28″   1 piece

Toenailing screws to the underside of your shelves will strengthen the structure.

THE MARKETS

This is another one of those unique pieces you can sell almost anywhere. I've never seen one in any of the furniture chains. It's also a great icebreaker. The price is such that almost any type of outlet, especially country stores or oak outlets, will take a couple to try. Make a couple from cherry or walnut, and even the fine stores will take them on. Be careful, though, about using expensive hardwoods on spec: Get the order first.

PRICING

Let's say you made this one from furniture-grade pine. There are some 22 board feet of stock in the project, at about 70 cents per board foot. So rounded up to the nearest dollar, we have a cost of $22. Add 10 percent for wastage ($2.20), and you have a total of $24.20. Multiply that by 5 and you have a wholesale price of $121. What could be better? Want to sell it retail? Simply add 50 percent, or whatever the market will bear.

Jelly Cabinet

This one is pure country. I include it because it's number five on my list of top-ten best-selling pieces. It's quick and easy to make—not to mention profitable.

CONSTRUCTION OUTLINE

The piece is made from furniture-grade pine finished to ¾″ thick; you could also make it from shelving board if you like. The construction of the carcass is achieved using through dados. The trim is attached to the carcass using glue and finishing nails; the nailheads are left showing. The doors are made from flat boards fastened to the carcass with Early American brass hinges. The piece in the photo has a painted finish, but you could use stain—either Early American, Puritan Pine or Provincial, all by Minwax—protected with a couple of coats of satin polyurethane.

CONSTRUCTION NOTES

STEP 1. Cut all the boards—sides, shelves, doors and trim—to size and run them through the jointer to true the edges.

STEP 2. If you have to build boards for the sides and shelves, now's the time to do it.

STEP 3. Set your table saw up with your stacked dado blade set to cut ¾″ wide and ¼″ deep.

STEP 4. Lay out the position of the rabbets and dadoes on the inside of the two

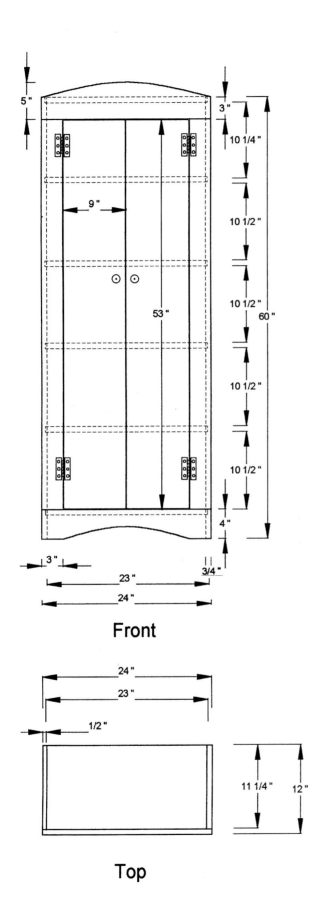

Front

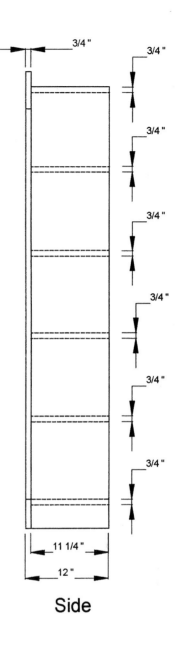

Side

Top

For the sake of accuracy, it is best to true the edges of all of your stock before you begin construction.

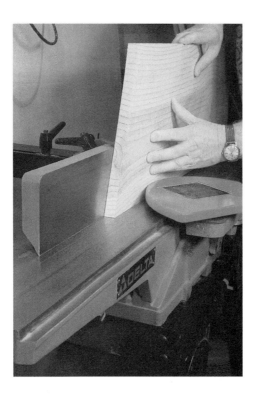

Cut the long curves for the top and bottom details on your band saw.

sides, spaced as shown in the drawing.

STEP 5. Mill the rabbets and dadoes.

STEP 6. Sand and stain all of the pieces prior to assembly.

STEP 7. Glue, assemble and clamp the top and shelves to the sides

STEP 8. Use #10 × 1¾″ screws and, from the underside, toenail the shelves to the sides for added strength.

STEP 9. Measure the diagonals to ensure the carcass is square. Make any necessary adjustments, and then set the assembly aside until the glue has fully cured, preferably overnight.

STEP 10. When the glue has fully cured, remove the clamps from the carcass and lay it on its back.

STEP 11. Use glue, finishing nails and clamps to fasten the trim to the front of the carcass, and then set it aside until the glue has fully cured.

STEP 12. Take the two panels that will form the doors, turn them face down on the bench and lay out the position of the cleats.

STEP 13. Use #6 × 1¼″ wood screws to attach the cleats to the doors; do not use glue.

STEP 14. Turn the doors face up on the bench, lay out the position of the knobs and drill the holes.

STEP 15. Attach the knobs to the doors.

STEP 16. Attach the hinges to the doors, and then fasten the doors to the carcass.

STEP 17. Apply a coat of satin polyurethane to all of the outer surfaces.

STEP 18. If you've decided on a painted finish, apply a sealer before you apply the paint.

PRICING

There are about 30 board feet of furniture-grade pine in this piece at a cost of about 70 cents per foot. Round that up to $1 per foot and multiply it by 30, and you have a cost of $30; add 10 percent to cover wastage ($3), and you come up with a total of $33. Multiply that 5 and you have a whole-

If you own a stacked dado blade, use it with your table saw to cut all of the rabbets and dadoes for this project.

sale selling price of $165, which is just about right. Sell it retail and you can add the usual 50 percent. This is a very profitable little item. It's a handy addition to any home—kitchen or living room—and thus sells well. With a little practice you can easily make three of these in a single eight-hour day.

THE MARKETS

This really is a country piece, which restricts the market somewhat. The ideal outlets for it are craft shows, craft shops or country stores. You might even find a trader in the local flea market willing to take one or two. Ideally, you should try to sell it retail. Advertise it in the local trader and you'll get lots of response. I've sold this piece in countless numbers; so should you.

MATERIALS

Sides

| 60″×12″ | 2 pieces |

Shelves

| 23″×12″ | 5 pieces |

Top Trim

| 24″×5″ | 1 piece |

Bottom Trim

| 24″×4″ | 1 piece |

Side Trim

| 53″×3″ | 2 pieces |

Doors

| 53″×9″ | 2 pieces |

Back

| 58″×24″ | 1 piece lauan plywood |

Country Bookcase

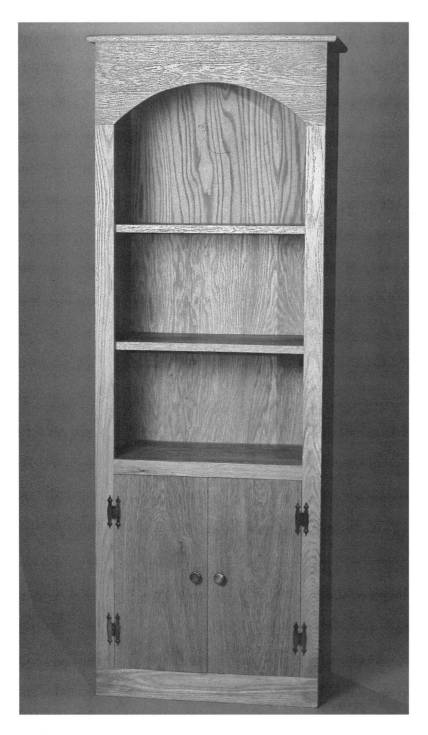

Made from pine, this is basically a country piece. Change it slightly and you broaden the marketplace. Build it from oak or one of the other hardwoods, such as maple, add raised panels to the doors and some classic crown molding, and you have a piece you could sell almost anywhere. I have one in my home. It's made from oak, and we use it as a curio cabinet.

CONSTRUCTION OUTLINE

As with most of the pieces in this book, the construction of this little cupboard/cabinet has been kept as simple as possible. The piece can be made from either oak or furniture-grade pine finished to ¾" thick. If furniture-grade pine isn't available, you can make it from shelving board. The shelves and top are dadoed and rabbeted to the sides; the trim is biscuited and glued to the carcass. If you're using pine, it can be glued and nailed to the front for a country look, in which case the nailheads should be left showing. The doors are simple boards with braces/cleats on the back sides to minimize warping, and the crown is no more than three pieces of stock with the front edges rounded over. The finish is simply a coat of stain and a coat of satin polyurethane. Although its construction is simple, almost to a fault, the result is both attractive and appealing. Not only that, but with practice you can

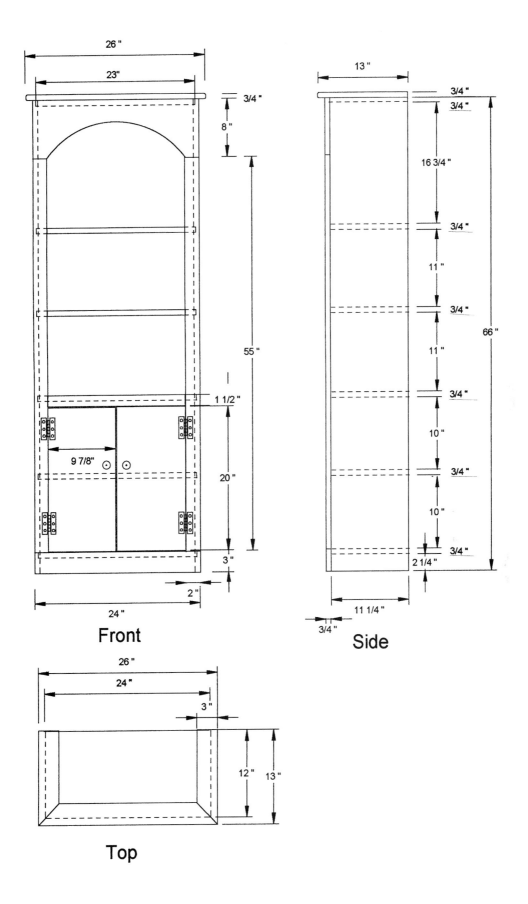

Front

Side

Top

It's easier to install a roundover bit into the router table and move the board through the bit than it is to move the router around the board.

With a smooth feed rate and a steady hand, the band saw is best for cutting these long detail curves.

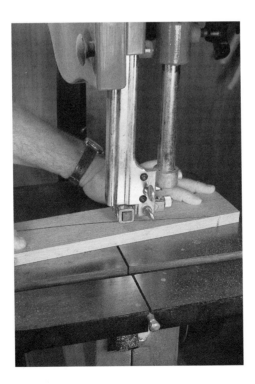

build as many as three of these in a single eight-hour day.

CONSTRUCTION NOTES

STEP 1. If you're using shelving board, cut all the boards—sides, shelves, doors, braces and trim—to size and run them through the jointer to true the edges. If you're using oak or furniture-grade pine, plane the boards to a finished thickness of ¾", and then run them through the jointer.

STEP 2. If you have to build boards for the sides and shelves, now's the time to do it.

STEP 3. Use either a band saw or a jigsaw to cut the detail for the top piece of trim.

STEP 4. Set your table saw up with your stacked dado blade set to cut ¾" wide and ¼" deep.

STEP 5. Lay out the position of the dadoes and rabbets on the inside of the two sides.

STEP 6. Mill the dadoes and rabbets.

STEP 7. Sand all of the pieces, including the doors, smooth and stain them prior to assembly.

STEP 8. Glue, assemble and clamp the shelves and top to the sides.

STEP 9. Use #10 × 1¾" screws and, from the underside, toenail the shelves to the sides for added strength.

STEP 10. Measure the diagonals to ensure the carcass is square. Make any necessary adjustments, and set it aside until the glue has fully cured, preferably overnight.

STEP 11. When the glue has fully cured, remove the clamps from the carcass and lay it on its back.

STEP 12. Use either biscuits and glue or glue and finishing nails to fasten the trim to the front of the carcass and set it aside until the glue has fully cured; if you're using nails, leave the nailheads showing.

STEP 13. Lay the doors back side up on the bench and lay out the positions of the braces.

STEP 14. Use four screws—no glue—to fasten each brace in position.

STEP 15. Turn the doors face up, lay out the positions of the knobs and drill the holes.

STEP 16. Attach the knobs to the doors.

If you are making more than one of these pieces of furniture at a time, you might consider setting up the radial arm saw with stops and a stack dado blade to cut the shelf dadoes. This will speed things up and ensure that all of the dadoes are in exactly the same position on all of the boards.

MATERIALS

Sides
66″ × 12″   2 pieces

Shelves
23″ × 12″   6 pieces

Top Trim
24″ × 8″   1 piece

Center Trim
20″ × 1½″   1 piece

Bottom Trim
24″ × 3″   1 piece

Side Trim
55″ × 2″   2 pieces

Doors
20″ × 9⅞″   2 pieces

Back
66″ × 24″   1 piece lauan plywood

Crown
26″ × 3″   1 piece
13½″ × 3″   2 pieces

STEP 17. Attach the hinges to the doors, and then attach the doors to the carcass.

STEP 18. Apply a coat of satin polyurethane to all of the outer surfaces.

PRICING

There are about 27 board feet of material in this piece. If you're using pine at a cost of about 78 cents per foot, you'll round that up to $1 per foot and multiply it by 27 for a cost of $27; add 10 percent to cover wastage ($2.70), and you come up with a total of $29.70. Multiply that 5 and you have a wholesale selling price of $148.50. If you're using oak at a cost of $1.20 per board foot, the wholesale price will be $297.

THE MARKETS

This is another piece you won't see in any of the great furniture chains, major outlets or fine furniture stores. Make the country version from pine, and your markets are craft shows, craft shops, flea markets and country stores. Make it from oak, and you turn it into a piece that could hold its own in any market.

Vegetable Bin

This piece is pure country kitchen, which means its markets are somewhat limited. Fine stores and galleries won't touch it; oak factory outlets might. Your best distributor will be country stores, craft shops, flea markets and, of course, retail. Even so, this has always been one of my best-selling pieces. I must have made and sold hundreds.

CONSTRUCTION OUTLINE

This piece should be made from pine, although I've made many from oak, which drives the price up to a point where they are difficult to sell. The back is made from a single piece of ¾″ stock, as are the sides and shelves. The two vertical doors at the front are made using lap joints; the top door is a single piece of ¾″ stock. The back, sides and shelves are fastened together using screws in counterbored holes; the holes are then plugged and sanded smooth. The screens that cover the inside aperture of the two vertical doors are made from black plastic rain-gutter guard stapled to the inner faces. The two front doors are held closed using magnets. The piece is finished with a coat of stain and a coat of satin polyurethane for protection.

CONSTRUCTION NOTES

STEP 1. Cut all the pieces to size and run the edges through the jointer.

STEP 2. Take the piece that will form the back and cut the shape to the top.

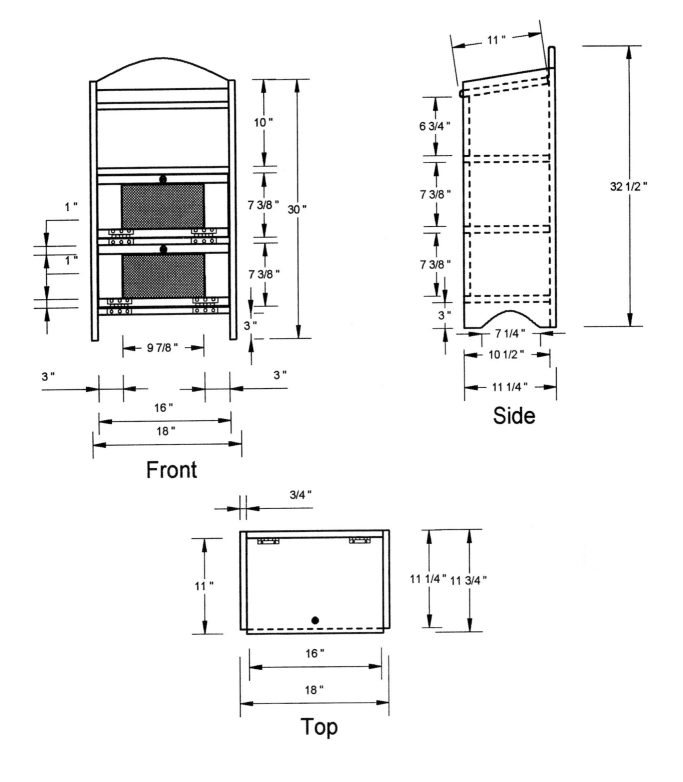

Front

Side

Top

Many times you'll find it easier and safer to use the jigsaw for decorative cuts on larger pieces. This is easier than trying to manhandle a large board through the band saw.

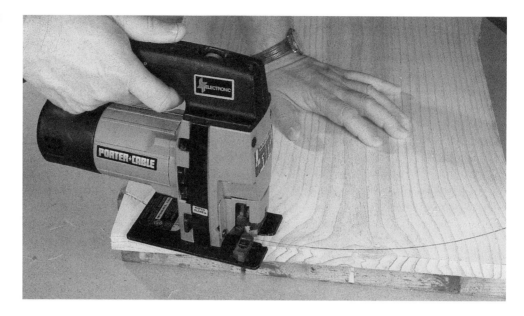

STEP 3. Take the pieces that will form the sides and cut the angle, 10°, to the tops, and cut the curved cutouts to the bottom edges.

STEP 4. Lay the two sides side by side on the bench, inner faces up, and mark the positions of the shelves as shown in the drawing.

STEP 5. Drill pilot holes through sides, inside to out, making sure that the holes are located central to the position of the shelves.

STEP 6. Drill pilot holes from the inside out along the back of each side and ⅜" in from the edges.

STEP 7. Mark the position of the upper front face and drill pilot holes from the inside out, ⅜" in from the front edge.

STEP 8. Turn the sides over so the outsides are uppermost on the bench.

STEP 9. Counterbore the pilot holes with a ⅜" bit.

STEP 10. Using #6 × 1¾" wood screws, attach the back to the sides, and then set and

Sand the butt joints smooth using the belt sander. Sand the edges first at 45° to the grain. Then finish-sand the edges along the grain. Don't be afraid to use a coarse belt—even as low as 50 grit—for the initial cuts. It will speed the job along and save you time. Just remember to be careful not to let the machine linger in one spot on the board.

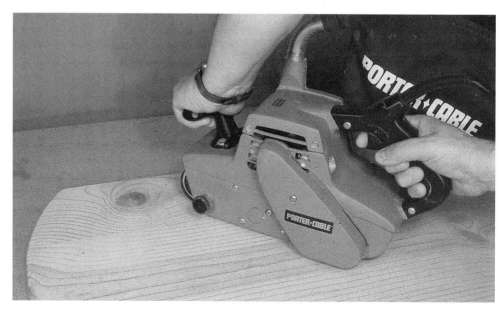

fasten the shelves in place, again using #6 × 1¾" wood screws. Do not use glue.

STEP 11. Set the upper front face in place and secure it using #6 × 1¾" wood screws.

STEP 12. Plug all the counterbores and, when the glue has fully cured, sand them smooth.

STEP 13. Build the two vertical door frames using lap joints and glue.

STEP 14. When the glue has fully cured, sand the door frames smooth and stain them.

STEP 15. Cut enough black plastic gutter guard (you can use wire mesh if you like) to cover the openings in the doors.

MATERIALS

CARCASS

Back

| 32½" × 16½" | 1 piece |

Sides

| 30" × 10½" | 2 pieces |

Upper Front Face

| 16½" × 6¾" | 1 piece |

Top Door

| 16" × 11" | 1 piece |

Shelves

| 16½" × 10½" | 3 pieces |

DOORS

Rails

| 16" × 1" | 4 pieces |

Stiles

| 5⅜" × 3" | 4 pieces |

Gutter Guard

| 11" × 6" | 2 pieces |

Hinges

| | 3 pairs |

Knobs

| 1" | 3 porcelain |

STEP 16. When the stain has dried, set the pieces of mesh in place over the inside of the openings and secure them using a staple gun.

STEP 17. The top door fits just inside, and parallel to, the tops of the two sides. It is held in place by hinges, and rests on the top edge of the upper front face.

STEP 18. Fasten the hinges to the lower edges of the two vertical doors, set the

This is one piece where it is OK to screw everything together without glue. Predrill pilot holes and counterbore them. Then fill or plug the screws.

On larger pieces you'll have no choice but to round the edges with a handheld router and a roundover bit.

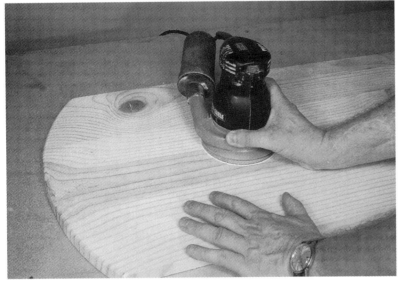

Do your finish-sanding with a good-quality random-orbit sander that leaves no swirl marks. Use a fine paper for final sanding—220 grit.

doors in place, and then secure the hinges to the two appropriate shelves.

STEP 19. Fasten magnet catches to the upper inside edges of both vertical doors.

STEP 20. Mark the positions of the knobs on all three doors, drill pilot holes and fasten the knobs in place.

STEP 21. Finish-sand all the outer surfaces, and then stain the piece inside and out.

STEP 22. Finally, apply a coat of polyurethane for protection.

PRICING

This piece won't make you rich, but it will provide an easy source of income. There are some 15 board feet of pine involved, at a cost of about 70 cents per board foot. This gives you $10.50. Add 10 percent for waste ($1.50), for a total of $12.00. Multiply that by 5 and you have a wholesale selling price of $60.

MARKETS

As I've already pointed out, the markets for this piece are somewhat limited, but rarely a week goes by that I don't get an order for at least two or three of these attractive, versatile and profitable little items. Country stores, craft stores, flea markets and even yard sales offer the best outlets. For retail, advertise the piece in your local trader.

Sofa Table

This is a neat little table, and I've had a great deal of success with it in various forms, always keeping to the overall dimensions. In its simplest form, it's quick and easy to make, and you can keep the price low enough to move it in large numbers. In its most extravagant form—with a drawer and turned legs—it becomes a very elegant piece indeed.

CONSTRUCTION OUTLINE

The version I've chosen for this book is the simple one. It has tapered legs and no drawer, and it's made from oak. The rails of the apron are fastened to the legs using mortise-and-tenon joints. The top is fastened to the substructure using buttons made from scrap stock and biscuits. The grain is filled using plaster of Paris and is sanded smooth. The finish has been left to look as natural as possible. I used Golden Oak Polyshades by Minwax.

CONSTRUCTION NOTES
Top

STEP 1. If you have to build your top from more than one piece of stock, select the boards. These should be at least 1″ thick, and quartersawn if possible.

STEP 2. If you're using rough stock, plane the pieces to the finished thickness of ¾″.

STEP 3. Cut all the pieces roughly to length: 40¼″.

STEP 4. Joint the edges ready for joining.

STEP 5. Lay out the boards ready for marking and joining; be sure to alternate the end grains to minimize future warping.

STEP 6. Mark the pieces for biscuits; each mark should 9″ to 10″ apart.

STEP 7. Glue, assemble and clamp the boards together, and then set the structure aside until the glue has fully cured, overnight if possible.

STEP 8. When the glue has fully cured, remove the clamps and then sand the top smooth using first 80-grit paper, and then 120-grit paper.

STEP 9. Using either a radial arm or table

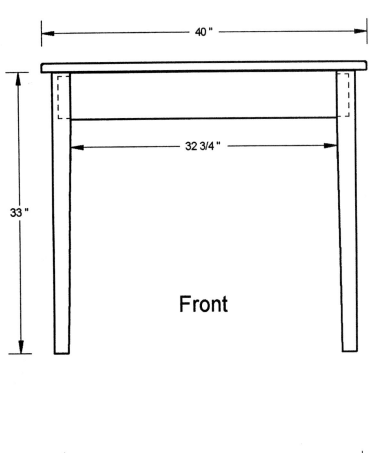

Front

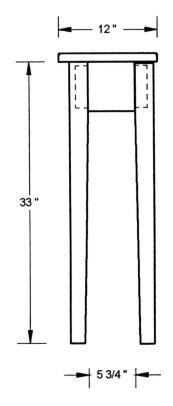

Side

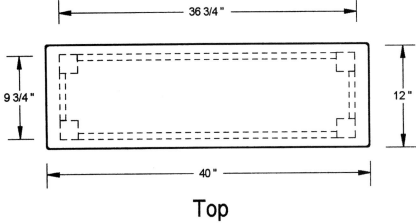

Top

Run the edges of all the pieces, especially the apron, through the jointer to true the edges and finish them accurately to size.

saw, trim the top to its finished length.

STEP 10. Mark a ½" radius on each of the four corners.

STEP 11. Use a belt sander to round the corners to the radius marks.

STEP 12. Using a ¼" roundover bit in your handheld router—or you can use your router table—round over the upper edge of the top.

STEP 13. Finish-sand the top surface and edges to 220 grit.

STEP 14. Use a creamy mixture of plaster of Paris to fill the grain, making sure to cover the end grains, and set the top aside to allow the plaster to fully cure, at least an hour.

STEP 15. When the plaster has completely dried, sand away the surplus material to leave the wood exposed and the grain showing white.

STEP 16. Sand the top to its final finish using 320-grit paper.

STEP 17. Finally, treat the top with your chosen shade of stain or, if you intend to use a stain-poly finish combination, set it aside until you're ready to assemble it to the subframe.

Legs

STEP 1. Cut your stock to make four pieces 33" long by roughly 2⅛" square.

STEP 2. Run all four pieces through the jointer to square them and give you your finished dimensions of 2" square.

The top of this table is small enough and easy enough to handle to allow you to run its edges through the router table to round over the top edge.

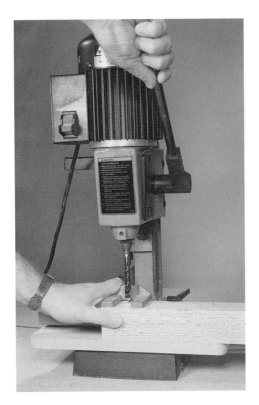

If you want to make money making furniture, invest in a dedicated mortising machine. These mortisers save a lot of time and effort over cutting mortises by hand. They will also increase the accuracy of your mortises.

A simple tapering jig, store bought or shop made, is what you need to taper the legs. Remember to taper the inside edges only.

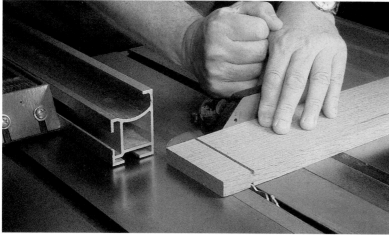

A professional tenoning jig is the best tool for making accurate tenons on the ends of the pieces that will make the apron.

or for turning if you've decided to use turned legs.

STEP 6. Set your tapering jig to 2½° and mill tapers to the two adjacent inside faces of each leg.

STEP 7. Fill the grain.

STEP 8. When the plaster is fully cured, sand to 320 grit.

STEP 9. Now, either stain the legs or set them aside until needed for assembly.

Apron

STEP 1. Take the four pieces of stock that make the rails of the apron and cut tenons, 3″ long by ⅜″ wide by 1″ deep, to both ends of each piece.

STEP 2. Dry-fit the apron to the legs and make sure that everything fits properly.

STEP 3. Disassemble the structure, glue, reassemble it and clamp it, and then measure the diagonals to ensure the structure is completely square. Set it aside until the glue is fully cured.

STEP 4. Finally, mill the biscuit slots to the upper inside edge of the substructure. These will be used to fasten it to the tabletop.

Button Retainers

STEP 1. From scrap oak stock, cut ten pieces 2½″ square by ¾″ thick.

STEP 2. In one end grain of each piece, mill a #20 biscuit slot, just as you would if you were going to butt joint the pieces.

STEP 3. Drill a ⅛″ hole through the center of each piece, and then set all ten pieces aside until you're ready to use them.

Assembly

STEP 1. Set the tabletop on the bench, underside up.

STEP 3. Mark the mortises, 3″ long by ⅜″ wide by 1″ deep, as shown in the drawing.

STEP 4. If you have a dedicated mortising machine, mill all the mortises as shown in the drawing. If you don't have a dedicated machine, cut the mortises by hand.

STEP 5. After you've cut the mortises, measure 6″ from the top end of each leg and make a mark for the start of the taper,

STEP 2. Place the top upside down on the bench; be sure to cover the bench with a soft pad of some sort to protect the finish.

STEP 3. Place the substructure in place on the underside of the top; measure the surrounding lips to ensure it's in the center.

STEP 4. Now take the ten 2½″ square retaining buttons, dry-fit a #20 biscuit to each one, and then slide them into the slots in the edges of the substructure. *Do not use any glue.* The top must be able to move as it swells and contracts.

STEP 5. Use 1¼″×#10 screws to fasten the biscuits, and thus the substructure, to the top.

Finishing

STEP 1. Do the final finish sanding to at least 320 grit if you're using oak—220 if you're using pine. Take your time over

These simple shop-made buttons attach the table-top to the apron.

MATERIALS

Top

40″ × 12″	1 piece

Apron

34¾″ × 5½″ (front)	1 piece
34¾″ × 5½″ (back)	1 piece
8¼″ × 5½″ (sides)	2 pieces

Legs

33″ × 2″ × 2″ (finished dimensions)	4 pieces

Table Buttons

2½″ × 2½″ × ¾″	10 pieces

this stage. The better the job you do, the better the final finish will be.

STEP 2. If you're using a stain-poly combination, now's the time to apply it. One coat should be enough; two if you have to lightly sand any raised grain.

MARKETS

This is a product that has a wide appeal and can be sold almost anywhere. Certainly country stores and oak outlets will snap it up, especially if the price is right. Fine furniture stores? Maybe, if you use cherry or walnut and turn the legs.

PRICING

There's very little lumber in this piece, only 6 board feet, in fact, plus the legs. So let's do this: Round the flat stock up to 10 board feet. The material is oak at about $1.20 per board foot, rounded up to $2 for a total of $20. The stock for legs costs about $2 each, say $8. So you have a total cost of $28, plus 10 percent for wastage ($2.80), for a grand total of $30.80. Multiply that by 5 and you have a wholesale price of $154.

Computer Desk

This is one of my top three best-sellers. Think about it. Today, more than 50 percent of the homes in America have at least one computer, and some of them more than one. Now, have you looked around at what's available in high-quality computer furniture? There seems to be only two levels: the high-end furniture sold by office supply houses, and the inexpensive, composition board furniture you can buy at the superstores. At the high end, you'll probably get a good-quality product, but you'll pay for it. At the low end, the usable life of the piece might be less than a couple of years, and that's only if you don't move it around. There's a real demand for good-quality computer furniture, especially if you're prepared to custom build. This one is compact, functional and lightweight, considering it's made from solid oak, has a rolling shelf big enough for a keyboard and mouse pad, and has plenty of room for the computer, monitor, printer, printer paper and any other goodies the user might want to store.

CONSTRUCTION OUTLINE

Construction is fairly simple. The piece is built in two parts: a lower desk unit and an upper shelf section. The bottom shelf of the desk unit is attached to the sides with stopped dadoes; the worktop is glued and biscuited to the sides, and the rolling shelf incorporates a simple set of hardware. The upper section is built using classic dado construction. The finish is a one-step, stain-polyurethane combination.

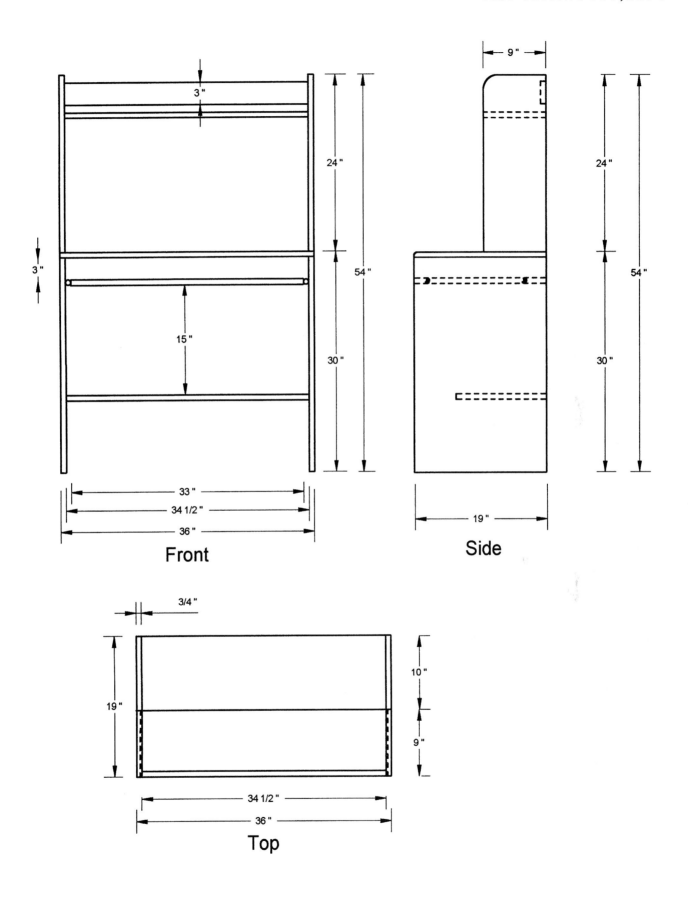

Front

Side

Top

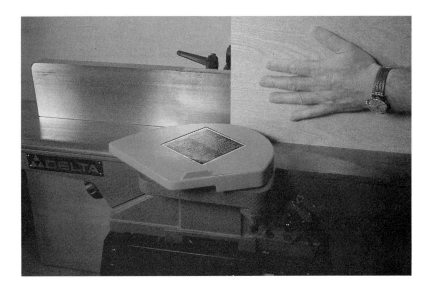

Be sure you true the edges on the jointer before you join any of the butt joints.

When making the butt joints reinforced with biscuits, lay out the biscuits about 8″ apart.

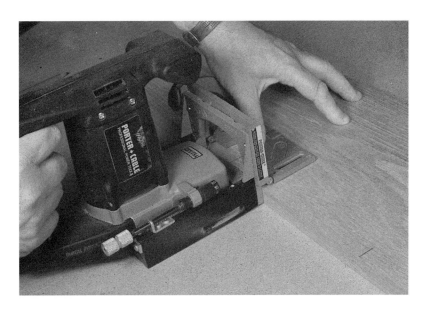

CONSTRUCTION NOTES

STEP 1. Cut all the pieces to size and run the edges through the jointer.

STEP 2. Carefully select the stock from which you'll build the boards that will make up the worktop, sides, rolling shelf and bottom shelf of the desk unit.

STEP 3. Lay out the selected boards and mark them for biscuits; they should be set about 6″ to 8″ apart.

STEP 4. Using a good-quality carpenter's glue, biscuits and clamps, build the boards that will make up the two shelves, the two sides and the worktop.

STEP 5. When the glue has fully cured, remove the clamps and sand both sides of each piece smooth to at least 220 grit.

STEP 6. Use either a proprietary brand of grain filler or plaster of Paris to fill the grain of all five sections of the desk unit.

STEP 7. When the filler has dried completely, sand away the residue and set the sections aside.

STEP 8. Take the two boards that will make up the sides of the upper shelf section, mark a 2″ radius to the front upper corners and then round them off. You can use your band saw to do this, or you can do it at the sanding center.

STEP 9. Take the two sides of the upper section and mill the dadoes to receive the shelf.

STEP 10. Mark the two upper section sides and the back for biscuits. You'll need two biscuits per end.

STEP 11. Take all four pieces of the upper section, sand them smooth to 220 grit, then fill the grain.

STEP 12. Using glue and clamps, attach the back and shelf to the sides of the upper section. Measure the diagonals to ensure the structure is perfectly square, make any necessary adjustments, and set the assembly aside until the glue has fully cured, preferably overnight.

STEP 13. Use your router with a ¾″ bit, set to cut ¼″ deep, and a T-square jig to mill the stopped dadoes to the inside of the two sides of the desk unit.

STEP 14. Mark the tops of the two desk unit sides and the worktop for biscuit slots. Mark for five slots set roughly 3″ apart.

STEP 15. Use glue and clamps to attach the

shelf and worktop to the two sides.

STEP 16. Measure the diagonals to ensure the structure is perfectly square, make any necessary adjustments, and then set the structure aside overnight, or until the glue has fully cured.

STEP 17. When the glue has fully cured, remove the clamps from the desk unit and fasten the outer sections of the metal slides, 3″ down from the underside of the workshop, to the inside faces of the sides, as shown in the drawing.

STEP 18. Fasten the two inner sections of the metal slides to the ends of the rolling shelf.

STEP 19. Set the rolling shelf in place and test to make sure the shelf moves smoothly back and forth on its rollers. If not, remove the shelf and make the necessary adjustments.

STEP 20. Do your final finish-sanding to 320 grit, and then apply at least two coats of a combination stain-polyurethane finish, sanding lightly between each coat if necessary.

STEP 21. Set the upper section in place on the lower section and make sure it stands perfectly square and does not rock or lean. You should supply a couple of small metal brackets to hold the two together and to ensure the top section doesn't slide sideways off the lower section. These need be no more than a couple of flat pieces of steel, ¾″ wide by 4″ long, drilled to take two #6 × 1″ screws. These would be fastened down the lower back edges of the sides of the upper section and the upper back edges of the lower carcass, effectively joining the two together.

PRICING

There are some 26 board feet of red oak in this piece. At a cost of about $1.20 per board foot, rounded up to $2.00, you have a total of $52.00 for your base cost. If you add the mandatory 10 percent for wastage ($5.20), you get a new total of $57.20. Now multiply that by 5 and you have a recommended wholesale price of $286; not

It's quicker to use a quart-size coffee can to scribe the radius detail than to fool around with a compass.

The band saw is the ideal tool to use to cut out this circular detail.

The table saw with a stacked dado makes quick work of the dadoes for the computer desk.

MATERIALS

UPPER SECTION	
Sides	
24″×9″	2 pieces
Shelf	
35″×9″	1 piece
Back	
34½″×3″	1 piece
LOWER SECTION	
Sides	
30″×19″	2 pieces
Worktop	
36″×19″	1 piece
Bottom Shelf	
35″×14″	1 piece
Rolling Shelf	
33½″×15″	1 piece
Hardware	
18″×¾″ metal shelf rollers	One set

bad for a piece made from solid oak. Add the usual 50 percent and you have a suggested retail price of $429, give or take a dollar or two. I've seen lesser pieces on sale for $550.

THE MARKETS

The markets for this piece are limited only by your imagination. I've sold desks like this one to independent furniture stores from the very small to the very large. The oak factory outlet is a natural, but I've also sold them to country stores, office supply stores, offices and, of course, direct to the public. This is a piece you can advertise in your local trade paper with confidence. As to selling direct to the public, if you can place only a couple of these at the right price, word of mouth will spread rapidly, and you'll soon be receiving repeat orders.

Entertainment Center

There's room for an entertainment center in every home; I have three in mine. We have one in the living room, one in my daughter's bedroom and one in our bedroom. Each one is different. The one in the living room is a corner unit; in my daughter's bedroom it's a reproduction of an eighteenth-century bachelor's chest; and in our bedroom it's a modern oak unit with four raised-panel doors, the one we're going to build here. I tell you all this to illustrate how many variations of the entertainment center there can be beyond the traditional design of the unit, where you have shelves of varying sizes and heights, and perhaps a door or two. The version described below I have sold consistently over the years, perhaps as many as 30, and it continues to sell well.

CONSTRUCTION OUTLINE

This entertainment center could be made from almost any clean lumber, especially from oak or pine. I've chosen red oak because it looks great, opens up the market and is popular with the buying public. I have made one such piece from cherry, but it was a custom order and very expensive. The sides of this unit are made from several pieces of red oak, thickness-planed to ¾″ and butt-jointed together using biscuits. The shelves, with the exception of the two in the upper cabinet where the TV and VCR will reside, are made from

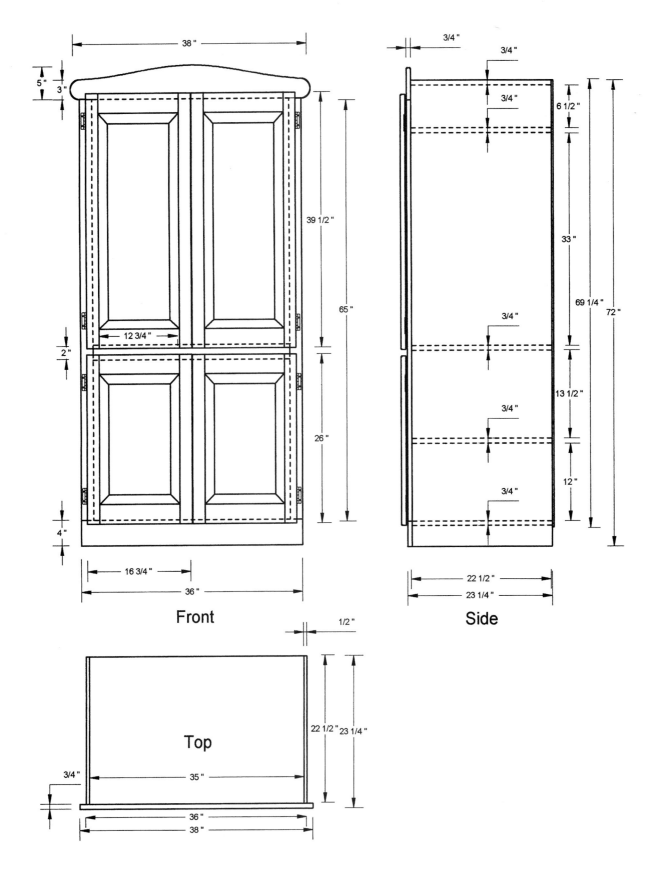

Front

Side

Top

¾″ pine stock; you could use ¾″ oak-faced plywood. I prefer pine because it helps to reduce the overall weight of the unit, which, even so, is very heavy. The other two shelves are made from ¾″ red oak. The shelves and top are dadoed into the sides and toenail-screwed from the underside for greater strength. The trim and doors are also made from red oak. The doors are of raised-panel construction using a router table with a panel raising bit and a set of rail-and-stile bits. As for the overall size of the unit, I've taken the most popular dimensions from my records. I think you'll find this size unit will serve you well. It will fit into a small van or pickup, and can easily be handled using a two-wheeled truck. You can, of course, alter the size up or down to suit your customers.

CONSTRUCTION NOTES
Carcass

STEP 1. First, select the board stock from which you'll build the two sides. It should be clean and fairly free from knots. Plane the pieces to the finished thickness of ¾″.

STEP 2. Run all the side boards through the jointer to true up the edges ready for joining, and then cut the ends square and to the finished length.

STEP 3. Lay out the boards for one of the two sides on your bench, making sure you alternate the direction of the end grains for future stability.

STEP 4. Mark the boards for biscuit slots— these should be 8″ to 10″ apart—and mill the slots.

STEP 5. Repeat the process for the second set of boards, and then glue, assemble

and clamp both sides and set them aside until the glue has fully cured, preferably overnight.

STEP 6. Now select the boards—pine and oak—you intend to use for the four shelves and the top and plane them to the finished thickness of ¾″.

STEP 7. Run all the boards through the jointer to true the edges ready for joining, and then build all five boards as described for the two sides. Set them aside until the glue has fully cured.

STEP 8. When the glue on the sides and shelves has fully cured, remove the clamps and sand all surfaces on all seven boards smooth to 120 grit.

STEP 9. Take the two sides and lay out the positions of the dadoes and rabbets that will receive the shelves and the top of the unit.

STEP 10. Because the sides are large and unwieldy, it's best to mill the dadoes using a T-square jig, a router and a ¾″ mortising bit set to a cutting depth of ¼″. Take special care to ensure that the dadoes run absolutely square to the edges of the boards, and that they are in exactly the same position on both boards. If not,

Because this is a large piece with very large sides, you'll need to reinforce the butt joints with biscuits. Set these 8″ to 10″ apart.

When using a rail-and-stile bit with a center bearing, you can line up the bearing with the back fence of the router table by using a straightedge.

you'll have problems squaring the carcass when you assemble it.

STEP 11. At this point it's a good idea to stain the shelves and the top completely, and the inner surfaces of the two sides; leave the outer surfaces of the two sides in their natural state for finishing later.

STEP 12. Place one side of the unit on blocks, with pads to protect the surface, on the shop floor, dadoes facing up. Glue and assemble the four shelves to the appropriate dadoes.

STEP 13. From the underside of each shelf, using #10 × 1⅜" screws, toenail-screw through the shelves into the side. Use three screws, equidistant from each other, for each shelf set.

STEP 14. Glue and set the other side in place on top of the four shelves already glued and screwed in place.

STEP 15. Make sure the shelves fit all the way into the dadoes; you can use clamps to pull them into place if necessary. The blocks under the lower side should provide space enough to insert the clamps.

STEP 16. Glue and set the top in place in the rabbets, and secure it with screws

driven through the top into the sides.

STEP 17. Clamp across the front and back to ensure stability while the glue is curing.

STEP 18. Toenail-screw the shelves to the upper side as previously described.

STEP 19. Turn the carcass on its back and measure the diagonals to ensure the carcass is perfectly square. If not, make the necessary adjustments and leave the unit overnight, or until the glue has fully cured.

STEP 20. Cut all the trim to size and plane it to the finished thickness of ¾".

STEP 21. Stain the inner surfaces of the trim, but leave the outer surfaces in their natural state for finishing later.

STEP 22. When the glue has fully cured, remove the clamps, set the trim in place on the carcass and mark for biscuit slots.

STEP 23. Mill the biscuit slots to the sides and trim, as shown in the drawing.

STEP 24. Glue, assemble and clamp the trim in place on the carcass. Leave the clamps in place until the glue has fully cured.

STEP 25. When the glue has fully cured, remove the clamps, clean away any surplus glue, and then sand the trim to 120 grit.

STEP 26. Sand all the outer surfaces to 220 grit.

STEP 27. If you're using oak, you'll need to fill the grain of the outer surfaces. You can do this now using either a proprietary brand of filler or a creamy mixture of plaster of Paris (as I do).

STEP 28. When the filler has fully cured, sand away the surplus filler using 220-grit paper in your orbital sander, leaving the grain now showing white.

STEP 29. At this point, all of the inner surfaces of the sides and trim, and all of the surfaces of the shelves and top, have been stained; only the outer surfaces of the carcass remain in their natural state.

STEP 30. Either stain the outer surfaces or use one of the new stain-polyurethane finish combinations to finish the outer surfaces of the carcass. If you use stain alone, apply a couple of coats of clear polyurethane, satin or glossy, to protect the finished unit.

Doors

STEP 1. If you haven't already done so, cut the pieces that will form the rails, stiles and panels, and then run them through the jointer to true up the edges.

STEP 2. Fill the grain and sand all the pieces to 220 grit.

STEP 3. There are two methods of panel raising you can use: The first, and most efficient, is to use your router table and a set of three bits specially designed to do the job. The second method employs both the router table and the table saw; I'll describe both methods, router table first.

from the router table and replace it with your panel-raising bit.

STEP 4. Make sure your panels are accurately cut to the finished size and then, making several passes and increasing the depth of cut each time, mill the outer edges of the panels until they fit properly into the grooves in the rails and stiles.

STEP 5. It's best at this stage to sand all of the door sections to a semi-finished state, and then stain the inside edges of the rails and stiles and the panels themselves.

Never try to run the end grains of a rail or stile through the table without using the miter gauge for safety.

When using a large panel-raising bit like this one, never try to remove all of the waste with one pass. It's best to make multiple passes, removing ⅛″ to ¼″ of material each time. Three or four passes with this bit would not be unusual.

Method 1

STEP 1. Set your router table up with the first of your rail-and-stile bits and then, making several passes and increasing the depth of cut each time, cut the combination faces and grooves to the inside edges of all the rails and stiles.

STEP 2. Next, set the router table up with the second of the two bits and cut the mating forms to the ends of all of the rails and stiles.

STEP 3. Remove the second rail-and-stile bit

STEP 6. If you have a set of Bessey clamps and door-building blocks, set them up to assemble the first door.

STEP 7. Using a good glue, assemble and clamp the door, and then measure the diagonal to ensure the piece is perfectly square. Set it aside until the glue is fully cured, preferably overnight.

MATERIALS

Sides
70″×20″ — 2 pieces

Shelves
35″×20″ — 4 pieces

Top
35″×20″ — 1 piece

Top Trim
36″×4″ — 1 piece

Bottom Trim
36″×4″ — 1 piece

Side Trim
64″×2″ — 2 pieces

Center Trim
32″×2″ — 1 piece

Lower Door Stiles
26″×2″ — 4 pieces

Upper Door Stiles
42″×2″ — 4 pieces

Door Rails
13¾″×3″ — 8 pieces

Lower Panels
13½″×20½″ — 2 pieces

Upper Panels
13½″×36½″ — 2 pieces

Back Panels
67″×36″ — 1 piece ¼″ lauan plywood

Knobs — 4

Sprung Hinges — 4 sets

STEP 8. Remove the clamps and do any necessary sanding.

Method 2

STEP 1. Cut the rails and stiles to length.

STEP 2. Using a ⁵⁄₁₆″ straight bit, set your router table to cut grooves ⅜″ deep to the center of the inside edges of the stock.

STEP 3. Take the rails and mill grooves the full length of the stock.

STEP 4. Take the styles and mill slots the full length of the stock.

STEP 5. Using a stacked dado head in your table saw, mill tenons ⁵⁄₁₆″ thick by ⅜‴ long to both ends of all eight rails. These tenons must tightly fit the grooves on the inside edges of the styles.

STEP 6. Using Bessey clamps and door-building blocks and clamps, glue the rails and styles together. Do one side only and dry-fit the other side, clamp it and make sure the structure is square. Set it aside until the glue has fully cured. Building the frame this way makes the final assembly of the door extremely simple.

STEP 7. Next, measure the opening, inside the grooves, to establish the true size of the panel.

STEP 8. Cut the panel to size.

STEP 9. Set your table saw to cut at an angle of 17°.

STEP 10. With a sacrifice fence at least 6″ tall, set the rip fence ¼″ away from the blade.

STEP 11. From the back side of the fence, use a piece of scrap stock to set the depth of cut of the blade so that the tip just breaks through the surface of the stock, leaving a step of at least ¹⁄₁₆″.

STEP 12. Mill all four edges of panel.

STEP 13. Remove the clamps from the rails and stiles and remove the un-glued stile, and then slide the panel in place.

STEP 14. Glue and clamp the single stile in place.

STEP 15. Finally, remove the clamps and do any necessary sanding.

Assembly and Finishing

STEP 1. Do any final sanding you feel is necessary, and then apply your stain-poly finish combination to the outer surfaces of the cabinet and the doors. If you've decided to use stain, apply a couple of coats of polyurethane for protection.

STEP 2. Mark the doors to position the knobs.

STEP 3. Drill holes for the screws and attach the knobs.

STEP 4. Attach the hinges to the doors.

STEP 5. Set the doors in place on the carcass and screw the hinges in place.

STEP 6. Stand the piece upright and check to see that the doors open and close properly.

PRICING

There are 40 board feet of red oak and 14 feet of furniture-grade pine in this piece.

At $1.20 per board foot, rounded up to $2, the cost of the oak is $80; add 10 percent ($8.00), for a total of $88. The pine rounded up to $1 totals $14; plus 10 percent ($1.40), totals $15.40. The total for the oak and pine is $103.40. Multiply that by 5 and you have a selling price of $517.00. Consider that a similar Broyhill entertainment center made from pine can cost upward of $1,200, and you see that your price for one made from oak is very reasonable. Sell direct to the public and you can add 20 to 50 percent, making it a very profitable item indeed. Using mini-assembly-line techniques, it's possible to build as many as five of these units over a single week.

The Markets

These pieces, made from oak or pine, will sell almost anywhere. Obviously, the oak outlet would be a logical choice, but any independently owned furniture store would buy them too. The market is limited only by your imagination.

TOOLS & MACHINERY

BALL & BALL
463 W. Lincoln Highway
Exton, PA 19341
Brass and iron hardware

BENNY'S WOODWORKS & TOOLS, LLC
P.O. Box 269
Bell Buckle, TN 37020
Inexpensive woodworker's supplies and
hardware

CHERRY TREE
P.O. Box 369
Belmont, OH 43718
Woodworker's supplies

DELTA INTERNATIONAL MACHINERY CO.
246 Alpha Drive
Pittsburgh, PA 15238
Stationary power tools

DEWALT TOOL COMPANY
626 Hanover Pike
Hampstead, MD 21074
Portable power tools

FREUD, INC.
218 Field Avenue
High Point, NC 27264
Cutting tools

JESADA TOOLS
310 Mears Boulevard
Oldsmar, FL 34677
Cutting tools, blades and bits

LEICHTUNG WORKSHOPS
4944 Commerce Parkway
Cleveland, OH 44128
Woodworking supplies and hardware

KLINGSPOOR ABRASIVES
P.O. Box 3737
Hickory, NC 28603
Abrasives

MEISEL HARDWARE SPECIALTIES
P.O. Box 70
Mound, MN 55364

NORTON COMPANY
1 New Bond Street
Worcester, MA 01606
Abrasives

PORTER CABLE
4825 Highway 45 N.
Jackson, TN 38302
Portable power tools

STANLEY TOOLS
600 Myrtle Street
New Britain, CT 06050

TREND LINES
125 American Legion Highway
Revere, MA 02151
Woodworker's supplies and hardware

WOODWORKER'S STORE
4365 Willow Drive
Medina, MN 55340
Woodworker's supplies and hardware

WOODWORKER'S SUPPLY INC. OF NEW MEXICO
5604 Allameda Place NE
Albuquerque, NM 87113
Woodworker's supplies and hardware

index